PARENTS
on a Mission

How Parents Can Win the Competition for the
Heart, Mind, and Loyalty of Their Children

CHITO,

It's BEEN GREAT KNOWING YOU,
GROWING WITH YOU, & WORKING OUT WITH
YOU. I HOPE IN THESE PAGES YOU WILL FIND
VALUE FOR YOUR FUTURE WITH YOUR WIFE &
CHILDREN.

RICHARD R. RAMOS

4/5/24

outskirts
press

Dedication

This book is primarily for parents, and those who will one day be parents. However, I also have a deeper purpose that I want to acknowledge. Although I am not directly addressing all the following issues, I still feel compelled to dedicate this book to all the children around the world that have endured abandonment, neglect, and abuse of every imaginable kind and have no voice to speak of the horrendous daily treachery they are victims of.

They live in the darkness of various abuses, kidnapping, trafficking, sexual exploitation, and even murderous sacrifices of religious rituals. If a child survives these tragedies, they are not lucky. Rather, they are destroyed...and have survived to carry their traumatic experiences with them for the rest of their lives. Sadly, I see no end to the child exploitation, neglect, and abuse we have all come to know. It causes me to wonder why this continues to be allowed by a loving and omnipotent God. It remains a mystery I will never understand.

Nevertheless, my desire and hope in writing this book is to strike at the root of this problem and be a voice for those forgotten children in darkness, to prevent other children from ever joining their life of silent misery.

I cannot save you, but I have heard you, and hope to speak for you in the place where it all begins...the home.

Proverbs 31.8-9

Table of Contents

- Orientation to the principles, core values, and concepts of Parents on a Mission.
- Four common principles of personal growth and emotional maturity.
- How to daily practice and implement personal growth principles.
- How to take control of how you think about yourself.
- How to reconcile past wounds, scars, and regrets, and heal present family relationships.

- Why and how to teach children the value of community unity in diversity.

- The Great Father
- Principles of Reconciliation
- Barriers to Reconciliation

- Loyalty is the "golden key" for preventing children from making negative lifestyle choices.
- How, why, and where parents are in a daily competition for the loyalty of their children.
- How to overcome and win the battle for loyalty.

Foreword

When I first heard about POM, my reaction was, why do I need this? I am the best parent I can be. I do not need to learn how to be a parent. I never believed that I needed to take a parenting class. My oldest son is seven years old with combined type ADHD; his father lives out of state. My youngest is a three-year-old whose father sees him when it's convenient for him. So basically, I am a single mother of two boys. Having a child with ADHD, I just thought the behavior comes with the ADHD. (Boy, I was wrong, I mean yes, he is still restless and likes to move 300 miles a minute, but his behavior has improved.)

I know in my past I have been a "partier," and my parents raised my oldest for about two years. I was there but not *really there*. I then decided it was time to grow up and I thought, "Hey, I know what I am doing. I don't need to learn anything. We will take it day by day." After experiencing POM my mindset has totally changed.

Before POM I had always felt bad for leaving my older son with my parents, so I would give in to everything he wanted, to try and make up for it. I thought this would make our relationship better, yet again, boy, was I wrong. I have learned and incorporated so much from POM into my home and it has become stronger and calmer. This class not only helped me become a better parent but most importantly it helped me learn about myself. After sitting in the class, I learned that this class was not there to teach me how to be a parent but to learn about myself and find the person I need to be so I can be a better parent for my children.

I truly enjoyed each week learning about leading my children in the right path in life, forgiveness of myself and past mistakes I have made, not living or disciplining with guilt, how to communicate not only with my children but with all people involved in the life of my children and myself. I also learned that I need to have a strong and healthy relationship with my children and by doing that I can be a better parent. I had never realized before that talking with my children and including them in decisions would make them feel more important in our family.

We have set family rules and decided on new traditions TOGETHER. When I let them choose some of the new rules for the house they were stunned. My youngest (who has an old soul) said: "Wait, Mom. I get to pick something?" My oldest also could not believe I was letting this happen. He said: "So, Mom, you won't get mad that I choose a rule?" His response stunned me. I was hurt to learn that I had made him feel I would be mad at him if he chose something to do. This really made me realize we needed to change things.

In the POM class I really enjoyed the POM Action Plans. These plans helped me focus on what areas I needed to work on. A few major accomplishments I have had with my family after utilizing some skills from POM were: 1) Knowing that it is okay to be stern, just doing it the right way, the same way, all the time. I have become more consistent and with this. My children respond better to me and do not throw tantrums when they do not get their way. 2) I have learned that talking to my children when they do wrong, explaining what was wrong about it, and giving them the chance to explain to me what they understood from the conversation, is one way that gives them the understanding to know that they have a voice, and I will hear it. This was a huge breakthrough for our family. 3) I learned that I needed to find out who I was, what I thought about myself, why I am here on earth and where I am going, and by doing this, I am not only teaching my children but also helping them be able to answer those questions about themselves.

This class has done a lot for me, not only as a parent but as a person as well. I have incorporated so much from POM into my house and it has made life a lot more enjoyable for my whole family, inside my home and outside my home.

I would like to mention I have a friend who took this class. She used to be all about herself and finding a "man ". When I would see her Facebook, it would be all about going to bars, or what a boyfriend at the time had done to her. She never really involved her children. Her parents had them the majority of the time. During and after she took POM, I began to see a change. I see more pictures of her and the kids doing things together. She now posts updates about milestones her kids have made, and I have not seen her even mention a "man" on her page. She has obtained a real job and is focused on working for herself and her children. This is coming from a person that unless you knew her well, you would not have known she even had kids. It makes my heart happy to see the changes in her life.

Amanda Cooper, Case Manager, Servicios de La Raza, Pueblo, Colorado

Introduction

The First Family is not in the White House; it's in my house!

As American citizens we have been raised with the concept that the "First Family" refers to the family of the President of the United States residing in Washington D.C. in what we call the "White House". This is an important honor we give the presiding President and his family as we recognize their leadership and position of authority, and convey respect for their family. Thus, when I say, "the First Family is not in the White House, it's in my house," it is in no way intended to disrespect or take anything away from the honor of the office of our President. Rather, it is an attempt on my part to use this well-known reference to catch the attention of parents and drive home a message about the importance of making their family the top priority and responsibility of their life. What could be more important? What can replace this awesome opportunity to raise children to become healthy, happy, positive, and successful adults that ultimately contribute to creating healthy and safe communities?

Secondly, I encourage parents to understand that they are not only raising "their kids," but they are also raising "our kids" as our families all share "our neighborhoods", attend "our schools", and befriend "our kids ". Therefore, the ultimate outcome of what goes on inside our homes daily directly relates to the condition of the safety and health of the larger community. After all, where do the citizens of the community come from? They come from our homes. Thus, the question is, what kind of citizens are we sending into the community, the neighborhood, schools, parks, and playgrounds every day? The fact is, the community is depending upon parents to raise responsible and respectful citizens that will make a positive contribution to the community as future leaders in business, education, religion, government, and a variety of other important roles that make up the community, the most important of which is being what I call a "parent on a mission". That is the subject of this book.

In my Parents on a Mission (POM) program I consistently encourage parents that they are the number one asset in the community. They are the most important persons in the community—not the police, pastor, priest, principal of the school, or politicians. Parents are in the best position to determine the health and safety of the community since it is they who have the future citizens under their care to nurture, discipline, and provide guidance during the most impressionable years of a child's life.

To illustrate the importance of the role of parents in the community, I am reminded of a conversation I had one day as I was attending a child's birthday party of a friend. The grandfather of the child was there and as we were sitting together, we had the following exchange:

"Richard, I want to ask you a question. A lot of kids in this community listen to you and with all the problems we are having with gangs and violence, why don't you get them all together and talk to them?"

"Well, that would certainly be helpful," I said. "And I have, and will continue to do that. But I don't think that is really the best way to handle this situation."

He looked at me, somewhat puzzled, and asked, "What do you mean?"

"Well, since you are a gardener by profession, let me put it to you in a way that I know you will understand. If you walked down the street in your neighborhood and noticed that the flowers in the gardens of your neighbors were all wilted, dry, and dying, who would you rather spend time talking to, the flowers or the gardener?"

With that a smile broke out on his face and he told me that I was right and had made a good point that he really had not considered before. I explained to him that our children were like the flowers in our gardens and the parents were like the gardeners and part of the problem in the community was that too many parents wanted me to be their gardener. I explained that this was too much for one person and that I needed help—I needed more "gardeners"—and if we really wanted to make the best and most effective impact, it would be done by talking more with the "gardeners" and not just the "flowers".

Thus, as we continue to search for answers to a number of issues regarding youth who are being heavily influenced by social media, music, and movies, as well as by the peer pressure of violent activity, drug and alcohol abuse, dropping out of school, teenage pregnancy, and other negative lifestyles, I suggest that the slogan, "The First Family is not in the White House, it's in my house" is a message parents need to hear, not only as an encouragement, but also as an exhortation for them to be *parents on a mission* to win the hearts, minds, and loyalty of their children for the benefit of having a happy family, as well as a safe and healthy community.

Through the POM curriculum, we are encouraging parents to consistently make every possible effort to invest their time, money, and relationships in their own home first, and thereby communicate to their children that they are the number one priority in their lives, which I contend will go a long way toward preventing kids from choosing negative lifestyles and rather to make positive choices for living a productive and successful life.

The "First Family" principle is something that parents can utilize free of charge, be culturally competent in, and have under their own control. Furthermore, when parents are exercising this First Family principle, they are implementing the best strategy for both prevention and intervention against children making negative lifestyle choices (1) by turning the hearts of children away from a destructive lifestyle and enabling them to soar in their natural abilities and become the kinds of sons and daughters, students, citizens, and eventually parents that anyone would be proud of.

As we have come to learn, youth that turn to join negative lifestyles, like gangs, are simply making a choice *to belong* as a substitute for parents and family life that all human beings desire to be a part of. (2) All of us have the same needs to be accepted as we are, loved for who we are, and given attention, dignity, respect, and self-worth. We all have a need for the emotional, intellectual, social, and spiritual parts of our lives being nurtured and built up to their inherent potential. It is this fundamental understanding that is often overlooked when looking for solutions for children and teens that have gone astray. The question usually is focused on "what they are doing," rather than on "what they are missing" that other "normal" kids, who live in the same neighborhoods, go to the same schools, and play in the same playgrounds, seem to have that troubled, delinquent kids don't have.

The firsthand experience I have gained throughout my career working with high-risk youth, gang members, and other delinquent youth has led me to the conclusion that is the thesis of this book: Parents—not more police, more policies, more playgrounds, more pools, more prisons or youth programs— are the number one asset in the community and in the best position to influence their children to choose loyalty to their family above loyalty to any number of other negative lifestyles.

This may seem too simple and obvious, but as I continue to examine and study these problems and talk with those involved with troubled youth and families, it usually comes right down to the parent-child relationship, or lack thereof, that is at the root of these problems. Thus, the term *"Parents on a Mission"* is an expression I came up with some years ago in an effort to *"turn the hearts of parents to their children and the hearts of children to their parents as the best practice for preventing kids from joining negative lifestyles."* This strategy begins with parents being inspired to take responsibility for their own personal growth in emotional maturity to address parent-child problems in the most practical, inexpensive, truthful, and caring way.

I began this effort after listening to the broken hearts of the students who were on my caseload when I was the "at-risk" counselor at two California schools (1990–1994). (3) I would leave every day burdened with what they were telling me. I would continue to ask myself: "What can I do?" "What is the answer?" "How can I really help these kids?" These questions led me to begin conducting home visits (on my own time) and that's where the light—the answer—came to me.

While in the homes of my students I clearly saw the lack of respect, strained communication, little to no control, and obvious dysfunctional relationship with their parents, stepparents, single parents, and grandparents who were raising their children's children.

I realize this perspective puts a lot of pressure on the parents. Nevertheless, I believe that pressure is what's needed to help parents take responsibility for their children, their life, their home, and not buy into the "It takes a village" mentality—a message that basically says parents do not possess the capacity to raise happy, healthy children on their own.

Although I understand this whole "village" proverb is well intended, it was meant for a different time, place, and culture. It's not the message parents need in today's culture of competition with 24/7 access to internet information, programs, and peers through social media.

In Parents on a Mission we teach, *it does NOT take a village to raise a child—it just takes good parenting.* Our intention is not to *blame* parents but to *name* parents as the most important people in the community. What we want from the "village" is help, but not control of our children. That is our responsibility. If we parents are willing to take part of the credit for the success of our children, we ought to be just as willing to accept part of the responsibility when our children fail in their social responsibilities as citizens of the larger community.

When children go astray, I never assume that the parent is a bad person, negligent, or abusive. But what I have found is many parents have simply never really learned many of the principles taught in the POM curriculum (which I will share in later chapters). Those who have learned these principles and practice them, in most cases, have healthy relationships with their kids, who are leading productive lives. These parents usually learned how to have a healthy relationship with their kids from their parents, or whoever was the principal person who raised them as children. Yet, all too often, many of us lacked parents who could demonstrate to us how to go about building healthy human relationships and thus we end up using the age-old philosophy of child-rearing: *"If it was good enough for me, it's good enough for you."*

In order to examine whether or not this age-old philosophy is a correct view to use in raising our children, we first need to look within and be honest about what the practices of our parents produced in our own emotional healthiness or unhealthiness. Next, we must look at what these "inherited" child-rearing practices are producing in our own children and their relationships with their siblings, relatives, teachers, friends, and authority figures—of which parents are the most important.

In her book, *The Drama of the Gifted Child, The Search for the True Self*, psychologist Alice Miller speaks to the need to look within as parents and be honest about our past:

> "Is it permissible, then, for me to take these keys and try to match them to the doors of an old house to discover a life that has long been awaiting to be recognized? It may be considered indiscreet to open the doors of someone else's house and rummage around in other people's histories. Since so many of us still have the tendency to idealize our parents, my undertaking may even be regarded as improper. And yet it is

something that I think must be done, for the amazing knowledge that comes to light from behind those previously locked doors contributes substantially toward helping people rescue themselves from their dangerous sleep and all its grave consequences." (4)

Related to this root issue of relationship with parents, is the issue of learning to respect the authority of parents. I have found this to be a vital foundational principle in preventing our kids from choosing negative lifestyles. For example, it is one of the things I have seen as a difference between kids who join negative lifestyles, such as gangs, and those in the same neighborhoods and schools who don't.

Contrary to popular belief, kids innately want to respect the authority of their parents and live in a healthy, happy relationship with them. But almost all the troubled youth I have talked with did not have it and were really brokenhearted about it. It became the hole in their hearts that they have tried to fill with gangs, drugs, alcohol, sex, and most recently their "identity," that just does not fill that hole, no matter how hard and long they have tried to fill it with these other things. I would even go so far as to say that kids who are successful in sports, academics, or other socially acceptable activities, yet don't have a healthy, happy relationship with their parents, also have that same hole or emptiness of heart, and nothing, not even "success," can fill it like the unconditional love and acceptance of a parent.

Many years ago, I was asked by a community group that was organizing a coalition to stop gang violence in South Santa

Barbara County, to come and speak at a community forum on the causes of acts of violence by youth. As we all know, the gang lifestyle, among other things, includes acts of violence. In fact, most initiations for gang membership include an act of violence called getting "jumped in", which is a short period of time (usually lasting a minute or two, or more in some cases) where several members of the gang beat up on the new member as a way of showing their toughness and desire to be a part of the gang. That is bad enough, but as we know, the violence does not stop there. Thus, as I prepared for my talk, I began to think deeply and draw upon all the knowledge and insight I had gained from listening to many gang members tell me their story and their reasons for doing the violent and destructive things they were doing.

The following is what I eventually came up with to share that day as my hypothesis for why kids commit acts of violence:

Acts of violence are caused by an angry heart. And an angry heart is produced by unresolved injustices that young people experienced as victims, usually in their own homes.

These "unresolved injustices" can range from sexual, physical, verbal, and emotional abuse and neglect suffered from any number of family members in the privacy of the home.

The above sentiment became a foundational theme I have spoken about, every chance I get, in my desire to help families and communities across the country address the issues of youth rebellion, violence, and dysfunctional family relationships.

I have found that this issue of unresolved injustices is also still a burden carried by many parents themselves. Their own issues of abuse have never been dealt with. Why? Simply because many parents either don't want to, or they don't know how. Thus, one of my main goals in POM is to encourage parents to take a moment to look inside their own hearts for their own unresolved emotional issues that may be what is preventing them from reconciling their relationship with their children. Of course, this emotional process takes time and is different for each individual parent. However, once this is accomplished, we can guide parents to then "turn their hearts towards their children" and find the strength to deal with unresolved issues their children may have been carrying in their hearts for years.

Again, this emotional process is not easy and can be very uncomfortable. But if we can find the courage to take this loving action, I know it will make a great difference in preventing and/or successfully intervening to win back our kids who may have gone astray.

I know this because so many youths have told me they wanted a better life and relationship with their parents, repeatedly, in juvenile hall, prison cells, letters, school classrooms, counseling sessions, and various other public and private settings I have experienced in my career.

As parents respond to the ideas, and consistently practice the principles and encouragement in this book, I am confident it will cause their children to turn their hearts towards their parents and cause a revolution of family reconciliation that will help, heal, and save more children from choosing a negative lifestyle than any other single factor. I have witnessed this process of reconciliation over many years as I have taught these principles and challenged parents to continue to be, or to become, *Parents on a Mission* by choosing to commit to the following principles:

1. Practice the principles of personal growth in emotional and spiritual maturity.
2. Practice the skills to earn and maintain authority over their children.
3. Be consistent in the proper use of discipline.
4. Build community in their home first as a means of developing good citizens that contribute positively to the larger community.
5. Learn, practice, and master the skill of reconciliation.
6. Take action to earn and win the loyalty of their children.

This book is specifically written for parents just like you on one of two fronts: 1) Parents of young children (infant to 12 years old) who might be worried about, or wondering how, to keep your children from going astray; 2) Parents who are burdened, struggling, heartbroken, because your children have gone astray and you are wondering what to do and where to go for help.

Perhaps you have experienced something that provoked your attention about your relationship with your children, and your inner voice is guiding you towards help and hope for your child or children who have become caught up in the spider-web of violence and other destructive behavior that is breaking your heart.

That inner voice has led you right here to learn about Parents on a Mission, which has helped so many parents across this country and internationally (Canada, Guatemala, El Salvador, Jamaica, and the Philippine Islands) win the love, respect, and loyalty of their children. Even parents who are incarcerated are being transformed and reconciling with their children before being released from prison and jail. (5) Here are a few examples:

"Dear Mr. Ramos, I would like to take a few minutes of your time to say "thank you" for introducing Parents on a Mission to the men here at Four Mile Correctional Center.... I'm an ex-gang member with seven children...after taking your Parents on a Mission class and the tools I've learned, it will help me become the great parent I want to be. I think that I speak for all the men that took the class when I say, thank you for giving us this opportunity."
–José

"Thank you for taking the time to implement this Parents on a Mission class here...I don't believe in co-incidences, so you were right on time in my life. Your story you shared with us of your personal experience with parents helped me tremendously. I will greatly *use what I have learned to establish a healthy family when I reunite with them soon..." – Joshua*

"I would like to say that this type of class is well over-due...POM's message to me was basically to "grow up". This class taught me that I need to accept respon-sibility, heal, and mend my relationship with my kids if I want to teach them how to live life...and not follow in my footsteps." – Charlie

"Dear Imani: I know that this letter may do very little to affect your life and deal with the resentment and anger you have towards me and my decisions that left me in prison and you fatherless...I hope that I can show through my actions that I have broke away from my past way of doing things and I'm trying to break through into a new future that includes a better rela-tionship with you. Maybe I can even earn your for-giveness in the process...if it wasn't for this class, I wouldn't even have wrote this letter because I don't know where to start. Just know that Daddy loves you and I regret my decisions but want to be proactive in finding a way to begin to fix our relationship." – Antoine (letter shared with permission)

I also wrote this book in response to a letter I received a number of years ago from a young girl crying out for help. I believe her letter is still indicative of many young people today.

"Mr. Ramos, the reason for this letter is that I'm pretty worried. You see, my brother is in a gang. He's 19 and about to get locked up for something that he did a couple of months ago. Me, I'm having problems with some girls in a gang too. I'm afraid to go out anywhere. Afraid I might meet up with them. But that's not really what I'm writing to you for. Recently some friends did something that scared me and made me realize that it's time to step in...I'm really tired of our raza hurting each other. I'm also scared for the younger generation. My little brother looks up to my older brother. What kind of a world do we live in?! I know one thing for sure; it ain't the one I want to live in. Mr. Ramos, I guess you could say this is a cry for help...you said you were gonna help our generation. That day in the church you really touched me. You made me realize there is a chance. It's hard to believe but I do believe the Lord loves us all and that he did not put us here to kill one another...all my life I wanted to do something special. Something that made a difference...I'd like to do something. I'm not sure what, but maybe a group of teens that feel the same way I do, to come up with ways to change this crazy world. I'm so scared, confused. I'm sitting outside on my porch looking out into the street wondering what it's going to look like in a couple of years if we don't do something. I pray every night before going to bed, but I feel the need to do something. God put me on this earth for a reason. Maybe this is it. I don't know, it sure wasn't to kill my sisters and brothers. I hope you've understood what

I'm trying to say. Please help, Mr. Ramos, we need to change our ways." –Con respeto, Irma

This cry from Irma (and for many other youth and families in this country and across the world), is why I am compelled to continue to write, speak, reach out, work, and train more POM parent mentors with the sincere intention of providing the strength, encouragement, guidance, and hope that can cause heart revelation, heart revolution, and home reconciliation of the peace, harmony, and love all families were intended to know.

Sincerely,
Richard R. Ramos
Santa Barbara, CA

Richard,

It's been a week since I completed Parents on a Mission Leadership Training. And I'm still savoring the information and content of the amazing training you provided. I use a lot of what I've learned during these two and half days in my daily life now and forever. The training left a beautiful and unexplainable feeling of accomplishment. Gracias!

The information and exercises done in the session are not only of benefit here at my job but, more important, with my family and friends and extended family. The class also afforded me the opportunity to validate my behavior and to feel comfortable with decisions made. And of course, it also taught me why I also made the wrong choices in my life. All good!

I know one thing for sure needed in my life is a Mentor. I have folks that I look up to, but it would be great to have a go-to person. I know the Creator will help me find one. I also, know what kind of Mentor I need. One that will guide/assist me to get to the PEAK of my life. Whereas, prior to taking the class it would just be to put things on a to-do list. Now my list has deadlines and will be updated on a weekly basis. I sincerely thank you for empowering all of us to get to our next level of being more compassionate and understanding folks in our daily lives.

From the moment you introduced yourself and started sharing "your story" you had my fullest attention. Each time, I found myself wanting to hear and learn more. I didn't even want the class to conclude or go on break. The simple and common-sense method learned is one of becoming responsible, caring, and loving parents when raising our children. Understanding the importance of parent commitment and being involved with children from the time they are born is essential and a must!! We want to have children that are good and abiding citizens. The knowledge obtained provided me a totally different way of looking at parents' and children's behavior. Thank you for allowing me to share my "story," and the trust for us to completely be open with one another.

I can't express enough how thankful I am to have taken your training and truly appreciate the enormous tools obtained during the training. I wish I would have had this training before becoming a parent. However, I am sharing what I've learned with my kids, grandkids, family, and friends and look forward to teaching the class in Spanish. May "Parents on Mission" be spread throughout the diverse cultures like wildfire. The end result will be a healthier community and more nurturing families throughout this world. What a Goal!! Si Se Puede!

– Maria B, Senior Organizer, CentroCHA nonprofit, Long Beach, CA

1.

Parent Personal Growth in Emotional Maturity

As long as you live, keep learning how to live. – Seneca

Each time before I begin teaching the POM curriculum, I always give a sort of warning, a heads-up, about what's coming by asking for the participants in the class (or training) for their permission to challenge them. Of course, not quite knowing what I mean by this, they always agree. And usually by session two or three they begin to understand why I asked them for their permission to challenge them because by this time we have come to that place of having to deal with self.

In various exercises they are instructed to look within themselves—something they are not accustomed to doing. Eventually, step by step, they begin to see their situation, their family, and their children in a new light, from an *inside-out* perspective. They make comments like, *"I thought I was going to learn about my kids…I thought we were going to talk about them and their issues not me and my issues."* I remember one woman, in a POM Colorado Department of Corrections training I was conducting, came up to me on one of the breaks and said, *"I didn't know you were going to make me cry."* Nevertheless, my experience over the years has been that parents appreciate this challenge. They appreciate the insights they gain about themselves and how their own relationship with their parents and family of origin has—and is still—affecting them and influencing their parental style of raising their children. Some of that is good…some of it not so good. Yet the exciting and empowering part is they then begin to realize that the solution to building or restoring healthy relationships with their children is within their power if they are willing to do the work to change and grow, which is what the POM classes are designed to do.

The reality is that personal growth in emotional maturity for many parents can be a very complex and deep, emotional process. Old wounds are difficult to heal. Old life experiences can be hard to recall. Old habits are not easily replaced, and old mindsets are not easily changed. In raising our own children we can easily get stuck in the "If it was good enough for me, it's good enough for you" mentality. But the challenge— the question—is, is it good enough? Was it "good enough" for you? And if it was, then you are a blessed individual that had an emotionally functional home where you received the emotional security, stability, and significance that is needed for all children. However, what I have experienced over the years of working with parents is that *the presence of our past in the present* was more of a hindrance than a help in raising happy, emotionally healthy children.

"...the strength and fruitfulness that trees exhibit above the ground is connected in the most direct and natural manner to that part of the tree that we rarely see. Indeed, a tree's root system not only formats its kind; it is the repository if not the presence of its past, as it grows through the generation-to-generation process of its limbs and branches. Most efforts to understand relationship systems recognize the impact of the past...The nature of connections in the present can have more to do with what has been transmitted successfully for many generations than with the logic of their contemporary relationship." (1)

This principle, personal growth in emotional maturity, begins with the awareness and recognition of the presence of our past in the present and is the key foundational principle that is so effective in transforming families.

As I like to remind parents when teaching and training, we *grow old* automatically, but we do not *grow up* automatically. Growing up requires intentional effort; insight, self-reflection, and the ability to take responsibility for one's own life, actions, and circumstances. It's a lifelong journey that must constantly be worked on from the inside out where character is built and loyalty to conscience becomes a habit. (Covey 1970)

Over the course of my career, I have found the lack of emotional maturity to be the *root* cause of many family problems, dysfunction, and alienated parent-child relationships.

To illustrate the importance of growth in our maturity level I like to refer to what I call living in our *peak potential*. Our peak potential simply means to live at the top of our human capacity—to live fully, to live our best version of our self; to be all we were meant to be, to experience our optimal life performance.

This thought of peak potential came to me one day as I was listening to Dr. Stephen R. Covey when he asked this question: *Is my personal potential greater than my life experience? Or am I living in my potential as my daily experience?*

That is a challenging question to consider in all aspects of my life. But what struck me the most at the time was how important it was for me to consider it from my perspective as a parent. It set me on a quest that I'm still on...and one I have been inviting hundreds (probably thousands at this point) to join me on as I seek to live in my potential as my daily experience, with the benefit of my family as my top priority.

In building family relationships (or any relationship for that matter), I cannot stress enough how important it is that we constantly give ourselves to this process of personal growth. When parents go into "automatic mode," thinking their age will automatically bring them the wisdom, strength of character, and emotional maturity needed, they will "flatline," meaning they stop growing. This is a major problem when having to deal with the daily work of raising children who have emotional needs and/or are not always as cooperative as we'd like them to be and require correct confrontation and/or discipline (more on discipline later).

The common problem this lack of growth creates is a case of the "blind leading the blind," except this is the immature leading the immature. In other words, when a 35-year-old parent with a 16-year-old mentality must deal with a 13, 14, or 15-year-old attitude, it usually doesn't go very well.

What an immature child needs is an emotionally stable and mature parent able to handle difficult situations without making it worse, which admittedly is not always easy to do. As I say in the POM Mentor training, (2) *Sometimes you fight fire with water. Sometimes you fight fire with fire. But you never want to fight fire with gasoline.*

I've been guilty of *pouring gasoline on the fire* myself more than I'd like to admit. Thus, I know of what I speak here. As parents we have plenty of opportunities to test our growth in emotional maturity as we are consistently faced with situations that call for a thoughtful, mature response, rather than a negative, quick reaction that exacerbates the situation.

Parent Power Becomes Our Weakness

When we lack emotional maturity and face difficult situations with our children, we usually end up *borrowing from our power*, which then *builds weakness in our relationship.* (3) Borrowing from our strength can mean I *react* by relying on my physical size to bully my kids. Or I react in anger and shout louder to overpower them. Or I use my intellect and argue my children into a corner, making them feel inferior and fearful of me.

Unfortunately, these types of situations are common and too often we make light of them. We rationalize our behavior and think it's no big deal that we shut down our daughter by yelling at her, or that we belittled our son and provoked him to anger and shame. After all, we tell ourselves, *I am the parent, they are my kids, and they shouldn't have done what they did to make me so angry.* But the hard truth is that reacting in anger, shouting, and exercising our parent power to get our way are the things that cause the bitterness, resentment, and weakness in parent-child relationships.

In borrowing from our power, we may win the argument, but we weaken and can also lose the relationship.

What is needed instead of the reactive borrowing from our power is a mature response. This means we exercise our *response-ability*. In other words, I have the capacity, the ability to respond to the situation, which requires utilizing the space between stimulus and response by thinking, reasoning, listening to conscience, and choosing a mature response instead of a quick defensive reaction. This requires practice and no one gets it right all the time (or at least I don't).

This is what I mean by living in our potential. When something happens to upset us, we have the ability as human beings to hesitate before we simply react to the situation. We have the capacity to stop, think, reason, and then decide or choose a more mature response, rather than a negative reaction.

Dr. Lindsay C. Gibson in her book, *Adult Children of Emotionally Immature Parents: How to Heal from Distant, Rejecting, or Self-Involved Parents,* says,

> "...when parents are emotionally immature, their children's emotional needs will almost always lose out to the parents' own survival instincts." (4)

To avoid the negative effect of borrowing from our power we need to recognize the difference between instinctual reactions for survival (like instinctively swerving out of the way to avoid a car accident) vs. instinctual reaction in relationships. The latter will in most cases weaken relationships. This is what Dr. Gibson is referring to above: when children lose out on their emotional needs due to the immature survival instincts of their immature parents in difficult situations.

Defining Emotional Maturity

Before we consider how to grow in emotional maturity, let's define what emotional maturity looks like. Dr. Gibson defines an emotionally mature person accordingly:

- Capable of thinking objectively and conceptually while sustaining deep emotional connections to others.
- Functions independently while also having deep emotional attachments.

- Differentiated from their original family relationships sufficiently to build their own life.
- Comfortable and honest about their own feelings.
- Get along well with other people, thanks to their well-developed empathy, impulse control, and emotional intelligence.
- Enjoy open sharing with others in an emotionally intimate way.
- Control their emotions when necessary.
- Use empathy and humor to ease difficult situations and strengthen bonds with others.
- They enjoy being objective and know themselves well enough to admit their weaknesses. (5)

My first encounter with the idea of emotional maturity came when I found the book, *Emotional Intelligence* (6), by the man most consider the godfather of the subject, Daniel Goleman. Since the release of his groundbreaking book the popularity of this subject has grown and he offers many books, articles, seminars, and any number of trainings to assist both professionals and the common mom and dad alike, wanting to improve their life on a personal level. It is the latter group that I am most concerned with for our purposes here. However, I highly recommend the book for those who want to learn at a much deeper and comprehensive level than I will cover in this book.

The vision for the Parents on a Mission curriculum is to develop parent leadership in the home. That is the crux of what we want to achieve: to build the parents' capacity to deal with anxiety they feel for the problems their children are having at home, school, and/or society in general.

The principles of leadership development have been studied for many years by various institutions, organizations, and individuals. It has become an industry with many different methods, theories, and philosophies on how to develop leaders in government, organizations, and various institutions. However, the idea of developing parental leadership in the home has not been given the attention I believe it needs and deserves.

For the most part, common parenting classes teach parents how to deal with, or fix, their children. They are taught to focus their attention and efforts on their children. What distinguishes POM from the conventional parenting classes is parents are taught to *fix* themselves…to focus their attention on their own past issues and upbringing that may be part of the problem they are having with their children.

> *"…If you want your spouse, child, client or boss to shape up, stay connected while changing yourself rather than trying to fix them." – Dr. Edwin H. Friedman*

The POM Medal of Honor

To begin the process of parental self-reflection, we start with what I call the POM Medal of Honor.

Our society does a fair job of recognizing and promoting as heroes and role models the sports star, rock star, and movie star. Recognition is also given to people in positions of social status like teachers, policeman, politicians, and the like. I'm not suggesting that these individuals don't deserve recognition for their accomplishments. But what I am saying is that parents, who do so much for their children in service and sacrifice, deserve just as much, if not more, recognition from society than they are usually given. Consequently, I've discovered that parents don't perceive themselves as significant players in their community the way they should. When I ask the question, "Who is, or are, the most important people in the community?" the answer I hear is not parents, but rather others like pastors, priests, principals of schools, politicians, etc. Again, I'm not suggesting these important individuals don't deserve credit and recognition for the services they provide the community. Yet, in my mind, and what I continue to emphasize is, moms and dads are the most important assets in the community, more than any other single individual or entity when it comes to producing safe and healthy communities.

Think about it. Where do the citizens of the community come from? Citizens go to church. They don't come from church. They go to school. They don't come from school. Citizens go to public places of service. They don't come from there. They're not produced and raised there. The fact is, citizens of the community come from our homes. And the question is: What kind of citizen are we sending out to the community every day? But I'm getting ahead of myself and will address that subject in a later chapter.

Let's get back to the POM Medal of Honor. Parents are provided a simple graphic that represents an emblem of a medal

(See Figure 1). The graphic has four quadrants where they are asked to write the following:

- Quadrant 1 – Write three positive words that describe you (or how you think your children would positively describe you).
- Quadrant 2 – Choose one word that best describes your greatest strength as a person and/or a parent.
- Quadrant 3 – List the services you provide your children on a regular basis.
- Quadrant 4 – List the sacrifices you have made (or would be willing to make) for your children.

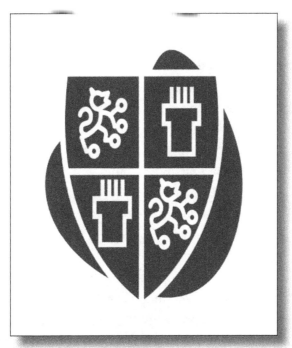

Figure 1

As you are reading this, I invite you (challenge you) to stop reading and do this seemingly simple exercise yourself and see how it goes.

What is always amazing to me is how parents struggle with this exercise—especially with the first two quadrants. Why? When we discuss this, it comes down to self-esteem or lack thereof. They don't know how to speak well or positively honor themselves. They are at a loss about how to describe themselves in a *good way*. They have never been asked to do such a thing. For some it is almost anathema to speak of oneself this way; it's bragging, bigheaded, narcissistic, and *not okay*.

To give a little encouragement I usually give some examples to get them going in the spirit of the exercise. For example, I'll write in the first quadrant that I am *generous, humorous, and understanding*. In quadrant two I'll write *understanding* and explain that I believe my children would agree with me that I am an understanding father, etc. These examples usually help them—give them permission—to speak of themselves this way and then we are off and running.

Once all have had a little more time to work on their medal of honor, I ask for volunteers to come in front of the class and share their medal of honor with the rest of us. However, I don't just let them come up and read the words. I probe and ask them to explain why they wrote what they wrote. This simple exercise is so powerful. It is truly an amazing process to watch as many get emotional, some break down, and others swell in a healthy pride to realize and be affirmed by the group that they are in fact important, significant, and a crucial part of developing the community because of the influence they are having at home with their children. They begin *to see* themselves differently. They begin to accept that they, like others who are given community recognition and honor, deserve it as well.

Next, we walk them through a four-step process to practice, on an ongoing basis, the principles of personal growth in emotional maturity.

Step 1: The Process of Self-examination— "Know Yourself to Grow Yourself"

- Make time to slow down, get quiet, and think, meditate and/or pray.
- During this time (maybe a ten-minute—or more—daily or weekly habit), practice listening to your heart and conscience: that still, small voice within.
- Practice "thinking about your thinking about yourself" by paying attention to your thoughts about you.
- Finally, when around others, pay attention to your self-talk, i.e., the words you say out loud about yourself. Are they negative, put-downs, self-doubting?

In addition to the above, self-examination also requires being authentic; a willingness to acknowledge my strengths and weaknesses, my moods and emotional inconsistencies, my likes and dislikes, my priorities and prejudices and a reaffirmation of my values. In other words, we need to be authentic.

Author, Michael Bess writes:

> "Know thyself," advised the Oracle at Delphi. Implicit in this adage lies an acknowledgment that humans possess a unique ability: the capacity to be fake. This is not so much a matter of deliberately deceiving other people...it has more to do with deceiving ourselves—coming to believe in a deluded fashion that we are someone we are not, or that we should try to become someone different than the person that we really are... Authenticity requires that we be critically aware of this slippery, dual nature of our personhood, and that we aspire to be more than just like a chameleonlike creature, constantly adapting our identity to conform to the external norms or models. Who is the real me? What are my deepest values and my most significant personal attributes? Am I living a life that reflects my inner nature?" (7)

Why is all this important? It's important because all our relationships with others flow out of our relationship with ourselves.

Signs of Growth in Emotional Maturity

How can I know when I'm growing? What are some indicators I can look for to measure my progress? The following is not a comprehensive list, but it does give some simple metrics we can easily be aware of.

I know I am making progress in my emotional maturity when:

- I find I have more self-control under stressful situations.
- Others (like my children) acknowledge that I am more patient than they have known me to be.
- I am more cooperative (at work, home, school). Even when I don't get my way, I still cooperate as a good team player.
- I am not as quick to speak my mind. I am more considerate about how what I say might negatively affect others.
- I am not as rigid in my attitudes. I am much more flexible in my thinking and receiving new ideas or ways of doing things.
- I am willing to acknowledge my mistakes and apologize without making excuses.
- I am more in control of my anger. I am learning to use it for the right reason, towards the right person, in the right place, at the right time, and to the right degree.

The process of learning to know oneself, while rewarding, can also uncover and shed light on things that are uncomfortable. It often exposes the fact that we have a negative self-image that can seem embedded and difficult, if not impossible, to change. The bad news is we have cultivated faulty thoughts, causing a negative self-image. The good news is our thought-life can be brought under our control and therefore we are empowered to change and transform the negative into a positive self-image. Here's one example:

> "Richard, I must say my way of thinking and approach to life and parenting has been forever changed by the recent POM training I received...on a personal level, I have been able to see where I went wrong, [and] made amends with my daughter and myself. I stopped blaming myself and simply named myself as the parent God created me to be. Thank you so much for this gift. It has taken me a long time to overcome my shame." – Rhonda Starr

Step 2: Know the Power of Your Thoughts

> "Research indicates that the average person—that means me and you—talks to himself or herself at least 50,000 times a day. And most of that self-talk is about yourself, and according to psychologist researchers, it is 80% negative—things such as, "They don't like me," "I'm never going to be able to pull this off," "That other team is going to kill us," "I'm always late, " "I can't seem to ever get organized." – Jack Canfield [8]

Oftentimes we wonder why we do or say certain hurtful things to those we love. To help discover answers to that question I encourage parents in this next step to practice *"thinking about our thinking about ourselves."* This is a process that can lead to discovering answers and healing unresolved wounds, shame, or guilt from our past that have not been dealt with and are at the root of hindering healthy relationships with our children. As author and leadership expert John Maxwell says, "Hurting people hurt people, and are easily hurt by them." That is a very telling statement that provides the kind of insight we need to help and heal how we treat others and ourselves.

Admittedly, peeling back the layers of years to examine our thoughts about ourselves can be challenging. Yet, it can also be very liberating to discover reasons why we think the way we do about ourselves and then understand that we can change our thinking as needed. If the above observation—I speak to myself about myself 50,000 times a day and 80% of it is negative—is accurate, then I need to do something to change all that negativity going on inside my brain.

Here's another quote I use to help emphasize just how powerful our thoughts are:

"Sow a thought, reap an action. Sow an action, reap a habit. Sow a habit, reap a character. Sow a character, reap a destiny." (9)

This little phrase is a simple but powerful formula for personal growth from the inside out; the point being that "sowing" actions, habits, and character ultimately leads to our destiny, and it all begins with our thought life: our thinking.

The fact is, sowing and reaping is a universal principle that works whether we understand it or not. But when we come to understand this principle, we have the power as human beings to use it to our benefit. In other words, we can control our destiny, change our current circumstances, and create a better life for our families, beginning with controlling our thoughts mostly about ourselves.

> "The main advantage of our intentional, internal thoughts is that we are the rulers of our inner realms. We decide what goes on. We are the dictators, queens, and kings...our thinking can offer us great strength or become a great weakness...we can use our thoughts to change our worlds for better or for worse. Thoughts can be creative or destructive. When we live inside a world of reactionary thoughts...we cede our power to other people...do you really want to be at the mercy of every person you encounter?"
> – Robert N. Stonehill (10)

How to Identify and Overcome Our Negative Thoughts and Self-Talk

There are basically two simple ways to identify the negative thoughts swirling around in our head:

1. **Give more attention and focus to your inner conversation and/or reflections.** For example, you wake up early in the morning and while lying in bed your mind just starts racing about a job or project you need to finish. Where does your mind go?

- You begin to have thoughts of stress, anxiety, doubt, fear, etc., rather than being happy, confident, and excited because you know you're going to *crush it.*
- You get a phone call offering you the opportunity you have worked for, hoped for, and said you wanted. But then you begin to wonder, *"Can I really do this job?" "Is this really the best thing for me?" "Is this the right timing to make this career change, and what will others think and say if I leave the security of my current job?"*

2. **Listen to your outward self-talk, the words you use about you.** For example, when someone gives you a compliment, how do you respond?
- "Wow, you really look great in that dress!" But then you say, *"Yeah, but it doesn't fit me right and I look funny in this color...don't I?"*
- "Hey, good job on your talk today!" But then you say, *"Thanks, but I forgot to mention some important points and then I got off-course and took too long...didn't I?"*
- "Did you get a new haircut and color? It looks great!" But then you say, *"It's okay, but I don't like it as much as I thought I would, and the color is a little off...don't you think?"*

If the above sounds familiar, join the negative self-talk club. But maybe you're thinking, *"Well, isn't that me just being humble?"* I don't know. Is it? That's the thing we are learning here. What we might pass off as humility could be how we deceive ourselves and rationalize our habit of putting ourselves down, doubting ourselves, and facing the hard truth that we really have a problem with our own self-image. And what I'm emphasizing here is the importance of exploring how that happens, and more importantly, what can we—should we— do about it?

Before I give you the answer of what to do about it and how to overcome this mindset, let me back up a moment and remind us about another question: Why is this important regarding parenting?

The simple answer is: If we realize that we don't have the relationships we want with our children and we want that to change, that change must begin with ourselves. We also understand that a solid, fun, healthy, and respectful relationship with our children does not always happen automatically. Thus, to *sow the seeds* and do the work to cultivate that healthy parent-child relationship, I need to acknowledge that all my relationships flow out of my relationship with myself. That's why this is important. That's why this inside-out process of emotional maturity is worth the work it takes to grow.

The growth exercise I'm sharing with you here to overcome negative thoughts may seem simple. But it is not easily mastered. It takes practice just like any new habit or skill. Nothing grows overnight. To overcome deeply embedded wounds of shame, guilt, self-loathing, fear, and other types of emotional hang-ups takes discipline and courage not to give in when that negative voice tells you, "*You're wasting your time and will never change.*" But, if you practice this simple exercise consistently, I promise you will experience personal growth and transformation.

Three steps to transformation from the inside out:

You must become:

1. A thought catcher.
2. A thought changer.
3. A thought replacer.

There you have it. Sound simple? Well, it is relatively simple in theory, but not in practice at the beginning stages. Yet anyone willing and wanting to change can do this and will experience growth in emotional maturity.

Let's go a little deeper into each of these steps:

1. Catching our thoughts requires focus, attentiveness, practice, and self-awareness.
2. Changing our negative thoughts to positive thoughts requires belief, discipline, and courage.
3. Replacing our negative thoughts into positive thoughts requires verbal self-affirmation. These are "I am" statements spoken out loud, so we hear ourselves affirm ourselves in the positive.

Some examples:

If I hear myself say to myself (either in my head or out loud), *"I'll never lose all this extra weight," "I'm a terrible mother," "I'm not good enough," "No one cares about me,"* etc:

1. I "catch" that thought because now I'm aware of my negative thinking and I know I don't have to accept it. I can catch and control my thoughts.
2. I change this negative thought to a positive thought in my mind first. I have an internal conversation…something like, *"No. I'm not accepting that about me. I am a good person and a good mother."*
3. I then say the positive self-affirming thought out loud to myself by making an "I am" or "I can" statement: *"I am a good person and a good mother,"* or something to that effect.

This may seem awkward at first. Talking to yourself this way. But I assure you it is a very powerful method of *self-talk* that will change your life if you persist.

Dr. Nate Zinsser is a well-known performance psychology expert who has spent the last three decades teaching soldiers, professional athletes, and executives the principles of mental toughness. One of the techniques he teaches he calls, "Getting in the Last Word". This is very similar to what I teach and explained above. He says:

"Dealing with your own internal negative thoughts, fears, and worries is very much the same—two competing opinions are vying for control of your mind and one of them is going to emerge as dominant...which voice will 'win the moment'? The one that speaks last and gets in the last word." (11)

For you to win in those moments it requires that you practice the three basic steps of: 1) catch the negative thought, 2) change the negative thought, and 3) replace the negative thought with a positive affirmation.

The Power of Our Words

Death and life are in the power of the tongue. –Proverbs.18.21

Remember the old saying, *"Sticks and stones may break my bones, but words can never hurt me"*? Nothing could be further from the truth. We all know how hurtful words can be. Some of you reading this book have been devastated by the words of a parent, relative, teacher, coach, or a significant other. Words can be our greatest weapon to build up another or to tear them down.

One day, when I was a young boy, my dad asked me what I wanted to be when I grew up. At the time I was probably about nine or ten years old. I was a huge Dodger fan as we grew up ten minutes from Dodger stadium in Los Angeles. My brother and I were pretty good athletes and played all the sports at the local park with other neighborhood kids.

Baseball was my favorite sport, and being a left-handed pitcher, I modeled everything I did on the mound after my boyhood idol, Sandy Koufax, the great Hall of Fame Pitcher for the Los Angeles Dodgers. So, when my dad asked me this question, I answered with the same aspirations that most young athletes have, which is to play in the big leagues. I said, *"I want to play for the Dodgers."* Now, think about the situation. Here I was, a young impressionable boy standing there waiting for my dad to encourage, motivate, and affirm my aspirations, as silly or as unrealistic as they might have been. But that's not what he did. He sarcastically said, *"Huh? Who do you think you are? Do you really think you're good enough?"* Crushing! Those *words* shook me and haunted me for a long time.

I'm not saying my dad meant to emotionally crush me (I really don't know if he meant to or didn't). Nevertheless, it did affect my mind negatively, tore at my self-confidence, and contributed to my being a very self-conscious person. Of course, I never understood any of that as I was growing up. I just intuitively knew I didn't have the confidence and faith in myself I needed as an athlete wanting to play professionally (I did almost get there anyway—another story for another time). But these words began to show up in other areas of my life. It took me years to overcome them, and I did this by practicing the very things I am sharing with you here.

By our words we move people to laughter or tears. With our words we can motivate a whole nation with an "I have a dream" speech. By the words in a song, the words in a book, or the dialogue in a movie, we can capture the hearts and imaginations of audiences both old and young alike.

So, why am I saying all this? Because I want you to realize why it's important for you to hear yourself say to yourself the positive affirmations in this exercise. Words are powerful! My words, their words, and your words. Therefore, use your own words to build yourself up on a consistent basis and do not give this power away to others when they try to bring you down, or when your own negative thoughts try to bring you down. Use your word weapons correctly and watch your life change.

Step 3: Use Your Power to Choose

"It has been said, 'Time heals all wounds.' I do not agree. The wounds remain. In time, the mind, protecting its sanity, covers them with scar tissue and the pain lessens. But it is never gone...I decided that I would not be overcome by events. My philosophy has been that regardless of the circumstances, I shall not be vanquished, but will try to be happy. Life is not easy for any of us. But it is a continual challenge, and it's up to us to be cheerful—and to be strong, so that those who depend on us may draw strength from our example... The most important element in human life is faith; If God were to take away all his blessings—health, physical fitness, wealth, intelligence—and leave me but with one gift, I would ask him for faith. For with faith in

him and his goodness, mercy, and love for me, and be-
lief in everlasting life, I believe I could suffer the loss of
all my other gifts and still be happy." – Rose Kennedy

All of us have faced challenges in life that overwhelm us emotionally and therefore steal our joy. We often allow these past
and current circumstances to dictate our quality of life. We
get caught up in what is commonly known as a *"victim mentality"*, meaning that we feel there is nothing we can do about
our situation. *"It is what it is,"* as they say, and we embrace
this idea that it's someone else's fault and/or someone else's
responsibility to do something to change or improve our situation. We live in a *"blame game"* bubble, always looking outside ourselves for reasons why we are unhappy, unsuccessful,
overlooked, discriminated against, and basically a *"victim of
circumstances"*.

To be fair, there certainly are people in power in this world
that are not fair, that do discriminate, and sometimes, in life,
we can be in the wrong place at the wrong time. Nevertheless,
the point I'm getting at here is that we don't have to accept
our circumstances as unchangeable or as something we can't
take responsibility for and decide to change the situation.
One such person who is a great example of facing the most
difficult of circumstances and deciding not to be *overcome by
events,* is Mrs. Rose Kennedy.

To most, if not all Americans, the Kennedy family needs no
introduction. Of the many things they are known for—politics, large family, wealth, and various scandals—they are

most known for the horrific assassination of President John F. Kennedy (1963) and his younger brother, Senator, Attorney General, and Presidential candidate, Robert F. Kennedy (1968). The Kennedy brothers were both gunned down in broad daylight for all the country (and world) to see. I was very young when both events occurred, but I do remember them (like those old enough to remember 9/11). I'm not mentioning these events to delve into politics or the who, what, when, and why of these awful tragedies. What I am getting at here is the heartache, grief, and devastating pain their mother Rose Kennedy (and family) experienced twice over. Yet, we read her words explaining that though the pain would never go away, she decided, chose, that she would not allow these events to control or define her life, because that would take away her example of strength in the toughest of times for the benefit of others: *"I decided that I would not be overcome by events…regardless of the circumstances, I shall not be vanquished, but will try to be happy. Life is not easy for any of us. But it is a continual challenge, and it's up to us to be cheerful—and to be strong, so that those who depend on us may draw strength from our example…"*

Viktor Frankl is another such example. In his book, *Man's Search For Meaning*, Viktor Frankl describes how he suffered years of torture and the worst of inhumane treatment as a prisoner in the Nazi concentration camps. His story is one of daily dread, depression, desolation, soul-destruction, and death all around him. Yet Dr. Frankl witnessed that even in the worst environmental conditions, man still has a choice of action.

"But what about human liberty? Is there no spiritual freedom in regard to behavior and reaction to any given surroundings? Is that theory true that would have us believe that man is no more than a product of many conditional and environmental factors—be they of a biological, psychological, or sociological nature? Is man but an accidental product of these....We can answer these questions from experience as well as on principle. The experiences of camp life show that man does have a choice of action....We who lived in concentration camps can remember the men who walked through the huts comforting others, giving away their last piece of bread....they offer sufficient proof that everything can be taken from a man but one thing: the last of human freedoms—to choose one's attitude in any given set of circumstances, to choose one's own way." (12)

This is an extreme example, to be sure, but nevertheless still relevant to the power we have as human beings *to choose* our attitude in the worst of circumstances.

I hope you find this human capacity we have, *to choose,* as enlightening and empowering as I do. It liberates me from the victim mentality. It proves that I can do something about my circumstances. Unlike animals, I can choose my thoughts and response to what happens to me rather than being controlled by my feelings and reacting instinctively like animals. If I'm not happy with how my life is today, I don't have to accept it. The truth is, where I've been in my past, and where I'm at in life today, may not necessarily be *"my fate,"* something that was always meant to be, especially if I'm barely hanging on and suffering through my daily existence. I can choose how to feel about and what to do about my circumstances.

In POM we teach parents we are meant to thrive in life, not just survive in life, and when it comes to raising my children and building my family life, I am not a victim of my past life. I can choose to overcome and create a better life for my family.

I want to end this section with a few principles to remember as we are learning how to know ourselves and grow ourselves in emotional maturity:

- My state of mind, or being, is not so much due to what happens to me as much as what I choose to do about what happens to me.
- I can choose how to feel about what happens to me.
- I can choose how to think about what happens to me.
- I am not my feelings. I have feelings but my feelings don't define me.
- I am not my moods. I have moods by my moods don't define me.
- Temperament is not destiny. My genetic and/or ethnic make-up does not determine who I become.
- I can choose to respond positively and not react negatively under stressful situations.

Step 4: The Power of Forgiveness and Living in Our Potential

"We must develop and maintain the capacity to forgive. He who is devoid of the power to forgive is devoid of the power to love. There is some good in the worst of us and some evil in the best of us. When we discover this, we are less prone to hate our enemies."
– Dr. Martin Luther King Jr.

As a young father I wanted to give my children the type of father I never had. But I had no idea how. I had no example of what being a good father looked like or acted like and besides that, I was only 24 years old. What could I know about parenting? As you can imagine, it didn't go very smoothly at first. At times, I found myself exploding with ugly and scary anger towards my wife and children. Then one night, I failed big-time. I went too far. I crossed a line. In a rage of anger, I lost control and slapped my wife. Immediately my heart was crushed. How could I be so stupid, to hurt the woman I loved so much? It was one of the most horrible moments of my life.

We had gotten into one of our rare arguments that just kept escalating louder and louder. I could feel the anger in me that seemed to overtake me every time I was about to get in a fight, or get made fun of, laughed at, or bullied in some way. I allowed it to get to that boiling point where you lose control and just strike and lash out, not caring in the moment the damage you might cause.

However, the bruised black eye on my wife's face served as a daily condemnation and reminder that I needed to figure out what was going on inside me—and change. I started to do some real soul-searching and asked myself, "Why do I get so angry? What's going on inside me that causes me to make such a drastic decision to actually physically hurt someone I love?"

You see, without realizing it, I was doing what a lot of people do by hanging onto unforgiving attitudes and resentment from my past. And, as Dr. John Maxwell says, "Hurting people hurt people." And after giving it much thought, I realized that a dead man (my father) was still controlling my life through my hard, resentful, and bitter heart towards him. I understood that much of my anger was a result of the injustices I had witnessed in my home as a small child and had never resolved in my heart. (13) I came to the realization that I needed to forgive my dad. Through this one incident I could clearly see the effect my angry heart was having on me. One night I had an emotional breakdown as I decided to let go of my anger towards him. Once I did, my life was transformed. I was free to grow, change, and become the kind of husband and father my wife and children deserved (an ongoing process, of course).

That was many years ago—and, no, I never hit my wife again. But I share that experience to offer you the hope and strength found in forgiveness, so you can be free to live in your full potential as a person, a married partner, and a parent.

When I teach about forgiveness, I always tell people that if they choose not to forgive, then they need to understand and accept the fact that they're choosing to live their life in an "emotional wheelchair". I know that sounds harsh, but this is serious stuff we're talking about here.

We've all seen someone who is living life in a wheelchair either because they were born that way or because some tragic accident happened that caused them to be permanently injured and therefore never able to live up to their *physical* potential. However, being born with a physical disability or having an accident is not a choice. But when we choose not to forgive, we are choosing that "emotional wheelchair," and we just need to accept the fact that we will never live in our full human potential that way. It's impossible.

Our emotional life is powerful and must be free to express itself and connect with other humans on a pure relational level. Just like it's (generally) impossible for a disabled person to live in their physical potential, it's impossible for an unforgiving person to live in their emotional potential, and this sabotages many, if not all, their relationships. So, again, I know that's a hard pill to swallow, but if it weren't so important for your personal growth and development, I wouldn't give it to you.

Having said all that, I realize the decision to forgive does not come as easy for some as for others. Fair enough. In cases like this I make these suggestions:

1. If you are in a place where you are simply not ready or able to forgive, then I suggest you at least begin to consider the act of forgiveness for your own emotional growth and health.
2. The next step is to simply seek for the desire—the willingness—to let go of the anger and bitterness. As you continue sincerely asking for and seeking the grace and strength to forgive and let go, it will come, and you will be set free.
3. Another reason people won't forgive is because they confuse forgiveness with trust. But these are two different things. Remember, forgiveness is free, but trust must always be earned. If you choose to forgive someone who has violated your trust, you will be free from resentment towards him or her, but they are still in your debt to earn your trust by proving their character over a reasonable amount of time. Forgiving someone doesn't mean you have to trust them too.
4. Another reason people are reluctant to forgive is they think that by forgiving their perpetrator they are *letting them get away with it* or endorsing their behavior. But the hard truth is, by holding on to your resentment, bitterness, and unforgiveness you are not only allowing them to get away with it, but also choosing to let him, her, or them, control your life and relationships. Thus, to encourage you to consider forgiving and letting it go, I ask you: Who is the one hurting and suffering by hanging on to a past you can't change? Once we understand that hanging onto unforgiveness is controlling and hindering our personal potential, we

come to understand that the choice to forgive is for our own good. To heal from past wounds and hurts, it helps us to make that liberating choice to forgive.

I can't think of a better example of the power of forgiveness than the life story of South Africa's best known and best loved leader, Nelson Mandela. If you're still having trouble with the issue of forgiving, I believe learning more about his story can help inspire you to look at things a bit differently. To put this in perspective, let me tell you a little more about his background.

As a young man he led his community in their struggle for racial equality. He was a founding member of the African National Congress and held many other positions in other organizations formed to win their battle against prejudice and discrimination. The fact is, his only crime was his opposition to the injustices of governmental racism, hatred, discrimination, and prejudice towards his people.

In the beginning of his struggle, he organized peaceful resistance in the form of civil disobedience. Later, when the peaceful resistance strategy was not working, he decided that the only choice left to him was armed resistance, for which he was eventually arrested and given a life sentence. In 1963, he was put into a prison cell to quiet his voice and end his threat to the government. However, his imprisonment only served to strengthen his voice of influence, as he became the most respected leader in South Africa while still in prison.

Years of civil pressure on the government to release him became overwhelming, and he was finally released from prison in 1990. Four years later, in May of 1994, he became the first democratically elected black president of South Africa.

After learning about all the injustices this man went through, no one would fault him for being full of hatred and wanting revenge on his persecutors. Once he came into power as the president of the country, we could have expected him to hunt down his persecutors and take his revenge. But Nelson Mandela was not your normal leader. He chose the path of peace and forgiveness instead. After being elected president, he said:

"From the moment the results were in and it was apparent that the African National Congress (ANC) was to form the government, I saw my mission as one of preaching reconciliation, of binding the wounds of the country, of engendering trust and confidence . . . I told the white audiences that we needed them and did not want them to leave the country. They were South Africans just like ourselves, and this was their land too . . . I said over and over that we should forget the past and concentrate on building a better future for all." (14)

In 2009, Mandela's life story was made into a movie, *Invictus*. If you haven't seen it, I highly recommend that you do. His actions of peace ended the decades-old racist policy of the South African government known as *apartheid*—a government based on laws of racial oppression and segregation. For his long life's struggle and political policies of peace and unity among all South Africans, he was awarded the Nobel Peace Prize in 1993, an award given each year to the person regarded as further influencing peaceful negotiations and relationships on a global level.

In speaking about how he felt about his enemies who had imprisoned him for all those years he said, *"To make peace with an enemy one must work with that enemy, and that enemy becomes one's partner,"* and *"Revenge is like drinking poison and hoping it will kill your enemies."* I just love that saying of his. It's such a liberating, life-changing, powerful truth.

Mandela experienced and understood what unforgiveness does to a person. Eventually, he discovered the freedom even a man in prison can receive from the power of forgiveness. He's an example for all who have suffered injustice, demonstrating how we can overcome anger and revenge towards those who have hurt and violated us and find the grace in our hearts to forgive and live in our full potential.

Along the path of our life, we are going to suffer being hurt by someone in one way or another. How we choose to deal with those hurts, however, is the key to whether we are a victim of our hurts or a victor over them.

Ultimately, choosing to forgive is an act of our will. It is not a feeling necessarily. It is knowing that if I want to be free and not live as a victim to my past that I must choose to let it go, forgive, and move forward to living in my full potential.

Principles for a lifestyle of forgiving:

- **Like any other skill, forgiveness must be desired.** The desire comes from my understanding that I'm hanging on to something that is causing unhappiness in my life.
- **Forgiving must be learned.** It is unnatural to forgive others who violate our trust or cause us physical or emotional pain. But once we see the freedom forgiving brings us, it helps us to make the decision to forgive even when our negative thoughts are telling us not to.
- **Forgiving must be demonstrated.** Showing forgiveness is one of the most powerful things a parent can demonstrate to their children. (15) The example of a parent forgiving their spouse, in-laws, siblings, and children goes a long way in building a happy, healthy home culture.
- **Forgiving must be nurtured.** As I said above, to forgive someone who has hurt me in some way is counterintuitive to our human nature. It is much easier to not forgive and justify our resentment. Therefore, unless we are continually nurturing this attitude it will continue to be a struggle.
- **Forgiving must be continuously practiced.** Because we live in an imperfect world, we will have plenty of

opportunities to practice and get better at letting go of the things other people do or say that cause us emotional suffering.

- **The power in the principle of forgiveness is experienced in three ways:**
    1. Being forgiven by someone you have offended.
    2. Forgiving others who have offended you.
    3. Forgiving self for past regrets and wrongdoing and/or hurtful acts you committed.

Personally, it's the third point that has caused me my biggest challenge. At times in my life, I have caused deep hurt in others that I care for and love and this can weigh heavy on one's conscience. It requires real sincerity and consistent faith to believe and accept forgiveness from others and from yourself. This is another reason why the work we do with controlling our thoughts and negative self-talk is so important. If we don't exercise our faith and accept that we are truly forgiven, our mind can condemn, ridicule, and cause us to become depressed with a very low self-image. This feeling of shame and/or guilt ends up affecting our relationships with our children, family, friends, and co-workers.

This principle of forgiving is so crucial and yet so overlooked as a major reason why families, parent-child relationships and other human relationships become so problematic, toxic, and dysfunctional. Furthermore, we all know that the behavior we model to our children makes a deep impression upon their character and behavior, especially in how they treat others. Demonstrating character that is unwilling to choose to forgive can become generational. It's an attitude potentially passed down to your children to justify mistreating others who make mistakes, err in one way or another, or fail to meet our expectations.

Finally, I want to express two important points to remember about forgiveness:

- The choice to forgive someone who has violated you does not require an apology. In my case, my father was long gone and yet I decided to forgive him without an apology from him or any other kind of acknowledgement from him of his wrongdoing towards me, my mom, and my siblings.
- Forgiving ourselves does not require that we receive forgiveness from those we have hurt. We cannot rely on others for our healthy relationship with ourselves. Guilt, shame, and blame are major hurdles we struggle to overcome because we think we need approval or affirmation from those we have offended. Not so. Ideally that would be nice. But the reality is, offended people are not always as gracious as we would hope them to be, and we cannot allow ourselves to be held emotionally hostage by their unforgiving spirit.

Everyone *sins*. No one is perfect and therefore no one has the right to hold another person in his or her debt for life as if they themselves have never committed the same or similar offenses to others. If you seek but don't receive forgiveness from someone you have hurt, do not allow that to be the defining factor for your own acquittal. Learn from your mistakes, seek the inner faith and strength to forgive yourself, and keep growing and moving forward.

> *"True forgiveness is letting go of a way of life…I learned that forgiveness is the most powerful and absolute required mental shift necessary to empowering our potential."*
> *– Dr. Eldon Taylor*

I end this chapter with two powerful examples of how the POM curriculum helps get people to this choice to forgive, and in some cases causes reconciliation.

I was teaching POM in the women's section of the Lerdo jail in Bakersfield. I had ended the session and challenged the class to write a letter, if needed, to express their feelings fully and put into use what they had learned about forgiving and letting go of the past so they could grasp on to a better future. When I returned the following day to teach, one of the women handed me a letter she had written as I had suggested. She wanted me to read it, so I did. When I finished reading it, I tried to hand it back to her, but she refused and said, *"No. I don't need it now. I'm free. I just wanted you to know how much this has helped me."* I asked her if I could keep the letter to use an as an example for others, to which she agreed. Here is what she wrote to her biological mother:

> I want you to know that I have never claimed you as my mother. The way I see it is you have never done

anything to earn that title. Allow me to explain. When you remarried a single man with three kids, making us all one big "Brady Bunch," I was only two years old, the youngest of us all. You never stuck up for me to either [the name of her stepfather] or his three spoiled, bratty children. They were always right. I was always wrong, so I grew up always being called a liar and never having a voice. Your desire to win their acceptance as wife and new mother was at the expense of never having a relationship with me. They were very cruel to me, and you were all I had to protect me, but you didn't. You are a coward. Even to this day you are still bowing down to him.

Luckily, my real father's girlfriend [Her name], stepped up to the plate and became a mother to me and I've been blessed to grow into the kind and loving woman I am today. That's why I'm writing you this letter. To release the anger I have been holding against you in my heart so I may grow more in maturity. I do have a love for you, because to be honest with myself I'm not perfect and have made many mistakes that I am now paying for, as I am sure you are also. So, I forgive you for it all, and will keep forgiving you daily as long as it takes. Sincerely, [Her name].

Now you might be thinking, "But Richard. If she gave the original letter to you that means her mother never received the letter from her." That's correct, which illustrates a point I made earlier about the power of forgiveness: to experience this freedom you neither need an apology or for the other person to be in your life. The power of forgiveness isn't dependent on others. It is an individual decision that liberates you whether the perpetrator is aware, alive, or not.

Here is another example of a son, after attending the POM classes in prison, expressing his feelings in a letter of forgiveness:

Dear Dad,

As a man at this point in my life I have learned to let go and forgive others for the wrongs they have done to me. I just wanted to sit down and write you to let you know how I feel about our relationship. And to build a proper healthy relationship, I feel it's important to share with you all that I feel.

That being said, I regret the way I used to behave in school. I understand that with the stress of work and the stress of supporting me and my sister, you had a short fuse and my behavior made things harder for you. You never really tried to talk to me about it. You always automatically got physical. This hurt, and at those times, and still even to this day, it feels like you hated me. Why did you lash out at me like that? Was it because you knew I was not your child?

When mom went to jail and CPS [Child Protective Services] took me, I still am angry and hurt that you left me in the system with no explanation for so long. You are the man who raised me. I consider you my dad. It hurts deeply that you would leave me behind and move on.

But this letter is not a hate letter or a boo-hoo letter. This letter is to let you know I forgive you and also to thank you. Because your discipline and rejection made me the man I am today. I will learn from our situation and your mistakes to be an excellent father.
– Sincerely, [His name]

Some things are harder to forgive than others. But to live freely, I must forgive. Some people are harder to forgive than others. But to live in my full potential as a human being, I must forgive. I urge you today to choose to live in your full potential!

The POM experience made sense. It put some things in perspective and confirmation...The biggest difference it made for me is that it showed me the importance of learning good parenting skills and the need to be "authoritative" and "understanding" as a parent.
– Resident, Limon Correctional Facility, Limon, Colorado

I think that POM experience is an eye-opener, especially for first-time parents.
– Resident, Limon Correctional Facility, Limon, Colorado

The POM experience opened my eyes to some relationships in my personal life that I need to make amends with in order to pursue future growth within myself and find peace in my family. A big thanks to you, Mr. Ramos. for creating this program and letting us use this in our facility.
– Staff member, Colorado Department of Corrections

Parents on a Mission is one of the most sought-out programs offered at La Vista Correctional Facility. I have seen this program completely change lives and redirect their thinking. I believe in this program 100%. It is an honor to be able to teach this class to our offender population.
– Officer Christina Aiello, Pueblo, Colorado

2.

Authoritative Parenting: How to Restore and Earn Respect for Parental Authority

"Don't demand respect, as a parent. Demand civility and insist on honesty. But respect is something you must earn – with kids as well as with adults."
- Anonymous

When I consider the issue of why kids go astray, I believe one of the most overlooked reasons for why this happens is the lack of, or misuse of, parental authority. Once again, usually when kids act out or make negative lifestyle choices, we tend to put our focus and efforts on changing their behavior, rather than looking in the mirror and asking if perhaps we are part of the problem. Of course, this requires the consistent practice and application of the emotional maturity exercises I covered in the first chapter. Many parents have either lost their child's respect for their authority, or they don't consistently and properly exercise it in the first place.

Author Lindsay C. Gibson says,

> "Emotionally immature people don't deal with stress well. Their responses are reactive and stereotyped... They have trouble admitting mistakes and instead discount the facts and blame others...they often overreact. Once they get upset it's hard for them to calm down..." (1)

One can imagine what happens with emotionally immature parents like this under the stress of disobedient, rebellious children who challenge their authority for any number of reasons.

Furthermore, parental authority has been undermined, diminished, and increasingly attacked as inappropriate in certain social settings. Examples include public schools instituting policies that keep parents ignorant of important subject matter being taught by the school, or life-changing decisions their kids are making with the guidance of school counselors on issues like gender identification, safe-sex practices, and/or abortions without parental consent. (2)

This undermining of parental authority has been a societal pressure on parents that just seems to keep growing in intensity. The parental voice of authority is being drowned out by schools, social service agencies, and government. Many parents are scared to exercise their authority with their children as they fear they might come under the scrutiny and judgment of these entities. They do not feel supported in exercising their rights to have a say in their child's education, discipline, social media exposure, and time engaging with peers over social media platforms.

In their book, *Hold On to Your Kids: Why Parents Need to Matter More Than Peers,* authors Gordon Neufeld, PhD, and Gabor Maté, MD state:

> "In today's world...parenthood is being undermined. We face insidious competition that would draw our children away from us while, simultaneously, we are drawn away from parenthood. We no longer have the economic and social basis for a culture that would support parenthood and hold its mission sacred...as modern parents we have to become aware of what is missing, of why and how things are not working in the parenting and education of our children and adolescents. That awareness will prepare us for the challenge of creating a relationship with our children, in which we, the caring adults, are back in the lead, free from relying on coercion and artificial consequences to gain our children's cooperation, compliance, and respect." (3)

One very clear message I teach in POM is that parents are not only the number one asset in the community, but they are also the final authority in the lives of their children. That is their rightful position in their home. It is their rightful position with their children in public, whether that be at the doctor's office, dentist's office, school principal's office, church office, or coach's office. This is a position of authority they should hold onto and never abdicate to other authorities in the community. Yet, sadly, many parents do exactly that due to the pressures mentioned above.

In POM we have a slogan that says, "It does NOT take a village to raise a child. It just takes good parents." When I first share this slogan people look at me strangely because most know the popular saying, *It takes a village to raise a child.* But does it really? Then I ask, "Well if that's true how many of you are willing to turn your child over to the village? The community?" Nobody ever raises their hand. I then go on to explain that this popular phrase, *It takes a village to raise a child,* is a good thought and well- meaning. The truth is, unfortunately, we are not even sure who we can trust anymore: the White House, the schoolhouse, the church house? Most certainly not the law enforcement house.

To be sure, what we do want from the community is their help and support. But the responsibility to raise my children belongs to me. Not the teacher. Not the counselor. Not the coach, pastor, or priest. That is the message we want to encourage parents with: You are the parent. You have the responsibility. And with the proper use of your authority, who knows—you just might raise a child who will raise up the whole community as we have witnessed before with individuals like Dr. Martin Luther King Jr., Cesar Chavez and many others.

On the other side of this coin, it must be said that obviously parents can lose their position of authority with their children if they, or their children, ignore the rules, violate social mores, and/or break laws that we are all subject to in a healthy society. This is all the more reason why the proper use of parental authority is so vital in raising obedient, happy, healthy, and productive children.

The Proper Use of Authority

While parental authority is vital to raising happy and respectful children, it is the proper and improper use of authority that needs to be addressed and understood by parents.

Many parents mistake *power* for authority, but they are two different things. Power implies coercion, and the ability to force someone against their will to do what you want them to do. In the context of small toddlers, whose tendency to do the wrong thing, say the wrong thing, and be in the wrong place at the wrong time endangers their well-being, employing your parental power for their own good is understandable. But as children grow in their understanding, it becomes necessary for parents to influence their children with their authority, not power. Authority is about influencing others to willingly follow or obey your instructions. This is what we want our children to respond to—not our parental power but rather our parental authority.

Three Basic Styles of Parenting

- **Authoritarian** – This is a controlling style with no room for discussion. The authoritarian parent does not allow or want input from children. The rules and expectations are what they are, and fear is the main tactic to get compliance. The child is not encouraged to express feelings or their point of view. The parents' decisions and actions are always right, especially when it comes to discipline.

- **Permissive** – A permissive parent is almost the exact opposite of the authoritarian. Much warmth and affection are given to children. However, the permissive parent refrains from offering guidance or direction. Children are left free to express their emotions, attitudes, and tantrums with no consequences. The parents do not see themselves in a position of authority or as someone responsible to shape character. They accept the child as is and allow children to regulate their own attitudes. They avoid confrontation.

- **Authoritative** – This style of parenting is a balance between the authoritarian and the permissive parent. They set high standards but also provide a lot of warmth, encouragement, and empathy when appropriate. As children mature, they explain and discuss their reason for their decisions and actions and include their children in house rules and disciplinary action as appropriate. They confront children, hold them accountable to family values and authority figures, and take an active role in shaping their character.

An authoritative style of parenting is what we advocate in POM as the proper use of authority that earns respect and obedience.

Authoritative parenting requires emotional maturity on the part of the parent, not the child. With an authoritarian style, parents are borrowing from their power. As I stated earlier, using this technique with older children, parents may get their way, but they will weaken their relationship and miss the opportunity to earn respect and obedience to their authority.

Benefits of Authoritative Parenting

Authoritative parenting establishes:

- **The foundation of moral character** – In the early years of childhood the parent's voice can be likened to the voice of a child's conscience. You are providing guidance, direction, and a sense of right and wrong, good decisions and bad decisions, and acceptable social conduct vs. unacceptable social conduct.
- **A sense of security** – When unfamiliar, unexpected, chaotic, and/or tragic things happen, our natural instinct is to look for assurance of survival and security. Any American who experienced 9/11 as a youth, teen, or adult remembers the state of the country when that tragic and dramatic terror attack took place. The country was shaken to its core. Normal major events like NFL games were cancelled and houses

of worship had record attendance (though this was short-lived). But what Americans were really looking for was a sense of security from those in authority, for the government and military to stand up and reassure us that we would get through this catastrophe and be okay. If we as parents have been exercising authority, nurturing, and guidance, our children will naturally look to us for security in times of disturbance.

- **Respect for the honor of others** – This is something that children must be taught. Whenever we had company over to our home, it was normal for our small children to pay no attention or give no recognition to our guests. This was an ongoing lesson I had to teach my children, especially when their grandparents would visit. I would have to call them in from outside or from out of their rooms and away from their video games just to come and acknowledge their grandparents, say hi, give a hug and a kiss, i.e., show respect and honor to our house guests. As my children got older this was their automatic response and I no longer had to "encourage" them. But I can tell you that this is not the norm of children in a lot of homes. Why? Because their parents have failed to exercise their authority; they have been too permissive on a regular basis and when it comes time for them to try and get their children to comply, the children ignore them. You see, the reason my children would respond to me about stopping what they were doing and come to pay honor to their grandparents (or whatever guests visited) was that I was consistent in exercising my authority on a regular basis.

- **Concern for the welfare of others** – This is another thing that children must be taught. Years ago, when one of my stepsons was about ten or eleven years old, I told him I wanted him to go across the street and tell our neighbor that from now on he was going to pull her big trash can down to the curb on trash day for her. He looked at me like I was crazy and said, "What?" Our neighbor across the street was an elderly woman and her husband had recently passed away. One day I saw her struggling to pull her garbage can down her driveway and onto to the street as we all do on trash day. So, I thought this was a good opportunity to teach my stepson about being a good neighbor. Did he want to do it? No. But did he do it? Yes. How—why? Because I was being an authoritarian parent? A mean stepparent? No. I was teaching him about being a good neighbor. Children must be taught to have concern for the welfare of others, and to do that I exercised my authority and explained to him why I expected him to do a kindness for our neighbor.

Respect for Parental Authority

Before I share some principles on how to earn respect for your authority, I want to take the time here to share a couple of caveats:

1. In order for you to earn respect for your authority it will require you to commit to practicing the personal growth principles I shared in Chapter 1. I cannot emphasize

this enough. This is the key to implementing all the six foundational principles I share in the POM curriculum. Knowing and understanding what to do is one thing. But the discipline of doing the internal work of personal growth in emotional maturity is quite another.

None of us are perfect and no parent gets it right all the time. That is an unrealistic expectation for parents raising another human being. Those of us who have experienced parenthood know that no two children are alike, even with the same biological parents. Temperaments, personalities, character, disposition, etc. are one way with one child and another way with another child. Although it is sometimes true that two children can be very alike in some ways, I would say that is the exception and not the rule. Therefore, I want to be clear on this point because too many parents beat themselves up, becoming disappointed and/or depressed when things don't go well, and they feel they are losing the battle of healthy child-rearing with one or more of their children.

The principles I share in POM are sound, but they are not a 100 percent guarantee that all will go well 100 percent of the time. But I do believe, and have experienced personally and with other POM graduates, that if you put in the time to practice the personal growth principles shared in POM (and/or all the other variety of emotional growth resources available in books, classes, and online courses out there), you are giving yourself a very optimistic expectation for raising happy, healthy, productive children. You are in the best position to influence and shape the character of your children and your growth in emotional maturity is the key.

2. Secondly, regarding respect for and obedience to your authority, I want to remind you that you have a head start with your babies and small children. I call it the "Home Field Advantage" (I will cover this in more detail in Chapter 3). But for now, I want to encourage you that, in my opinion, children inherently desire to love, respect, and obey their parents. Why wouldn't they? They are with us from Day One receiving attention, affection, and love. As the natural process of daily life unfolds, parents and children form the family bond of a strong emotional attachment that meets the need that all human beings have, which is to belong—to be a valued member of the family. As children grow, they instinctively know they need support, guidance, rules, discipline, and care. Having said that, the mistake we can make sometimes is taking the innate desire for granted, not realizing that this desire still needs to be cultivated, nurtured, and brought to fruition. How that is done is what I want to share with you next.

Principles for Earning Respect for Parental Authority

It is important to realize that although our children will misbehave, they will also want to reconcile and know they are secure in our unconditional love. However, reconciling is not something most young children will know how to do unless we model and communicate this with them. One adage I teach parents is: "When our children do the wrong thing, we must do the right thing." Of course, the "right thing" can mean many different things depending on the situation. But, in general, what I'm expressing here is that the misbehavior of our children offers us the opportunity to exercise our emotional growth, to respond in appropriate ways rather than emotionally reacting in ways that can make the situation worse. Remember: fighting fire with water and with fire can be effective, but we never want to fight fire with the emotion of *gasoline*.

Principle number 1: Decide that a good relationship is more important than being right.

After a confrontation parents have an opportunity to set the example of humility. To exercise humility will usually take some time to cool down and rethink how we have handled the situation. The truth, oftentimes, is that the way we have handled the confrontation was not good. We are at fault for the words we used and how we reacted to a difficult situation. Or, even after rethinking it all we may still conclude that we were right. Here is where we need to be aware of choosing to be stubborn because insisting on being right does not always build relationships, and that is the more important point.

The more important issue is restoring a healthy understanding with our child. We can achieve this through a calmer communication as an attempt to reconcile our difference regardless of who is right or wrong.

Some parents might not buy into this and reject this with an attitude of, "Too bad, they will just have to get over it." But oftentimes our children don't, and this stubborn attitude can cause our child to harbor resentment and begin to disrespect us, not because they think they are always right, but because we do.

Usually, kids know when they are in the wrong. However, what they are reacting to is our disrespect for their views and a devaluation of their child development process. Thus, for relationship's sake I suggest you:

- Calm down and think beyond who is right or wrong and consider if there was a better way to handle the situation.
- Go back and listen again to their side of things and make sure they feel heard and understood. Remember: understanding their point of view does not mean we have to agree.

These actions build relationship and respect, and they help you maintain your role as the primary authority figure in their life. Most kids will respond to this type of exercising of authority and respect us for our humility, fairness, and willingness to hear them out. The clear message this sends is how much we value them as individuals and how much we want a healthy and meaningful relationship with them that goes beyond having to be right.

Principle number 2: Admit when you are wrong and apologize.

After practicing the art of listening, we may discover that we were in fact wrong in our thoughts, words, and deeds—plain and simple and no excuses. Again, this is why our emotional maturity is so important, because oftentimes our mistakes as parents are a result of jumping to wrong conclusions.

After we listen to our kids under more emotional control, we know they are right and only our pride will keep us from admitting to ourselves, and to them, that we were in the wrong.

Another way we can come to realize that we were wrong is when our conscience begins to bother us because of the way we handled a situation with our child.

For example, there were times when I would get into it with one of my children. Arguing, yelling, saying things out of anger, slamming doors, etc. (maybe you know what I'm talking about?). Once the argument ended, I would go sit down and either begin to read, or watch TV, or just find something else to do. But in the quietness of those moments, that *still small voice,* i.e., my conscience, began to talk to me saying, *"You didn't handle that well. You didn't listen to your daughter. You lost your temper again and you need to go back, apologize, and make this right."*

Now at that point I had a decision to make. Either I was going to listen and obey my conscience—or I wasn't. And the worst part about it was that even if I shrugged it off and just continued to do what I was doing, that still small voice wouldn't go away...not right away.

This is a prime example of what I'm referring to about emotional maturity and why my continuing on the path of personal growth is so important. Emotionally immature people don't listen to their conscience. That can be dangerous, because if you choose to continue to ignore your conscience, you end up dulling its voice, leaving you to your own immature mind, which is not a heathy place to be as a parent if you care about living in your full potential and building a healthy family culture.

Emotionally mature people respond to their conscience and do what it takes to make things right. Here's a personal example:

I recall one time after my three oldest kids had become teenagers that I needed to apologize for some of the mistakes I had made with them as I was in a time of personal growth and could see that they were beginning to resent the way their two younger siblings were benefiting from it. I was more patient, understanding, lenient and flexible. At that time, we lived in a small apartment with a cozy living room where I asked them to join me for a talk. I began by sharing my heart and apologizing for what they had to experience with a younger and less experienced father. I know I was not abusive, but overly strict and intolerant in ways that I knew had probably wounded their hearts in some ways. As I turned to my oldest son and apologized for disciplining him too harshly at times, he began to break down and cry. Until that moment I had not realized how much I had wounded his heart. By his reaction to my apology, he had obviously been carrying this in his heart for some time. I could see and felt the healing that was taking place in his heart towards me and all I could do was hug him and cry and apologize. Up to that time, we had a good relationship, but after that I know it was deepened and better than ever before and remains so today. (4)

Once we know that we were in the wrong it's time for the humility to look our child in the eye, admit to them we were wrong, apologize, and ask for forgiveness. When children witness authority figures admit to their mistakes and apologize for them, it goes a long way in establishing a respect for you and ultimately your authority.

Principle number 3: Be flexible, fair, and firm.

Know the difference between mistakes or accidents and defiance or willful disobedience.

As parents sometimes we can be guilty of "choking on the ant but swallowing the camel". In other words, we make the little things big and the big things little. For example, as our children get older, they come under more peer pressure to fit in, be cool, and join the "in crowd" as we used to call it back in the day. Now your daughter has graduated from elementary school and is in middle school. One day she comes out of her room to go to school, and you hardly recognize her. Her hair is different. Her clothes are different, and she is wearing facial makeup. In other words, she's growing up and is trying to fit in with her friends and other girls her age at school. But that's not how you see it. You're surprised. You react in anger. You start yelling and saying hurtful things about how she looks, and demand that she go back to her room, change her clothes, and take off the makeup. Embarrassed and humiliated, she runs back to her room in tears.

The next day you're watching TV, and you overhear your wife tell your daughter to wash the dishes. Your daughter gets upset and says she doesn't want to. Now mom gets upset and starts arguing with her. Eventually in the heat of the moment, your daughter refuses to comply, tells her mom to "shut up," and storms out of the kitchen. And you…do nothing and say nothing. Now which of these two incidents is the "ant" and which is the "camel"?

Is the reality of my daughter growing up and trying to find her way amongst her peers the bigger issue? Or is it the tone of voice she uses towards her mother and talking back to her in such a disrespectful manner? In the first scenario, you saw this as a major issue to the point of verbally putting your daughter down and humiliating her to tears. In the second scenario, you saw this as no big deal and just sat there continuing to watch TV as your wife, her mother, was disrespected by her daughter…no big deal, right? I don't think so.

Don't get me wrong. I understand that our children might go too far at times when they are under peer pressure to fit in. And at that point we can intervene and provide some parental guidance. A young girl changing her hair style and clothes and putting on makeup is a normal stage of growth. And not wanting to do house chores and talking back to a parent is a normal (for some, not all teens) stage of growth as well. Now this may not be the best example, but you tell me. Which is "choking on the ant" and which is "swallowing the camel"?

We may differ on the answer to that question, but I think you get my point. I suppose one could say that a change in hair style, clothes, and makeup doesn't fall under the category of a mistake or accident, but certainly refusing to obey a parent asking a child to do their chores and then talking back in a disrespectful manner is willful defiance that in my view cannot go unchecked by a parent and deserves a firm response and potential consequences. The former issue, in my opinion, is an opportunity for flexibility and a fair discussion to show our teen that we understand, we've been there, and we just want to be sure they don't take it too far, a message most teens will understand when it is delivered in a calm manner.

Kids are very tuned in to unfairness or injustice and have a keen sense of what is a mountain and what is a molehill. I believe avoiding unfairness or injustice when dealing with our kids is a matter of maintaining a flexible and fair posture. This takes perception, insight, knowledge, and experience but it also requires the ability to listen to your kids to learn how to discern different situations. The key here is that kids know that you have the final word, yet you are allowing them to judge themselves, and this is where you can gain respect, earn loyalty, and create emotional bonds that pay big dividends later down the road when it counts. Through being flexible, fair, and firm we open the opportunities to develop character, deepen the relationship, and take hold of moments for a lesson in leadership and the proper use of authority.

Thus, the battle for establishing respect for parental authority is a must and must be handled correctly, consistently, fairly, and firmly.

The Parents on a Mission curriculum is a transforming agent for the young men and women in our community. Countless lives have already been changed for the better and affected for the future by being exposed to this material. Although now, I currently do not have any children of my own, I know what incredible influence I have on my nieces and nephews, younger siblings, neighborhood children, and numerous children that I encounter daily. I also know the impact I have on the lives of the young men I meet in the Justice Population while working in the County Jail. Through these meetings I harness the opportunities to enlighten them about the Parents on a Mission curriculum and encourage them to apply the principles to what POM identifies as being a responsible, nurturing parent that raises good citizens. The Parents on a Mission "train the trainer" course coupled with the Leadership Packet has rekindled my desire to make a greater impact not only in my own personal life but to become a much greater life-changing agent throughout my community. I am deeply honored and excited to be able to bring so much HOPE to those who need it the most. Thank you.

Daniel D. Lopez
Outreach Specialist
Garden Pathways, Bakersfield, Ca.

3.

The Home Field Advantage

Three Secrets to Raising Children
Who Say "No" to Peer Pressure

I developed this strategy out of the need to give parents an answer when they would ask me, *"Mr. Ramos, how can I prevent my younger children from following in the footsteps of their older brother/sister that is already... "* Then they would describe whatever negative lifestyle one or more of their older children were involved in: drugs, gangs, dropping out of school, rebellious and/or violent behavior at home or at school, etc. They feared their younger children would also get involved and they wanted to prevent this. But I didn't have an answer.

As I mentioned earlier, at the time of being the at-risk counselor at the school, I was a young parent myself. I hadn't experienced any of my children going astray, so I couldn't really give any credible counsel and that bothered me...a lot.

I would go home and think about it. It was one of those things that keeps you up at night. I didn't want to give some unrealistic, corny advice, yet I knew there had to be something I could come up with that was realistic, based on the same principles I was using with my own kids.

I did some research and discovered that most kids who go astray do so between the ages of twelve and fifteen years old. That caused me to have one of those "ah ha" moments. I thought, if that in fact was true, that kids' greatest risk for making bad choices began at the age of twelve. That meant parents should have a twelve-year head start before their *competition* steps on their field.

Having been an athlete, I tend to think in sports metaphors. And the more I thought about it, the more I saw the temptations and peer pressures for this time frame as the "competition". The twelve years before the competition became a threat where an advantage parents should have, to win the battle of peer pressure –IF they knew what to do during this crucial time frame. Thus, I call it the "Home Field Advantage" since most of the time small children, from infancy to twelve years old, are under the care and influence of their parents at home.

If you are not a sports fan, here is a brief explanation: Having the home field advantage is important in giving an edge to winning a game, especially big games like a playoff or championship game. Being able to play on your home field, with most of the fans in the stadium on your side, and being familiar with the nuances of the field (or court) you practice on every day, can give you an edge in the competition of a game, not to mention the fact that the referees are on your side, too. (That's kind of a joke...but then again, referees are human. I'll just leave it there).

I then thought through a time frame of twelve years and not only what parents must do, but also *how* to do what they must do to maximize this twelve-year window of opportunity. I broke up the twelve years into three different time frames:

- Infant – two years old
- Two years old – five years old
- Five years old – twelve years old

The question I answered for parents was, what should be happening in the life of a child during each of these key time frames? The following is what we teach parents in the POM classes.

Secret # 1: Parents are Gardeners of the Soul. Time Frame: Infant – two years old.

I like to use the term, "gardener" because it speaks to the skill of nurturing and cultivating that is vital for a child's well-being, especially during this specific time frame.

Infants, toddlers, and pre-school children have no concept of negative lifestyles – therefore there is no competition...yet. But parents must seize this time frame to cultivate, nurture and ground the roots of the soul during these most impressionable years. Even before a child is born, studies have shown that embryos are aware of their environment and that parents who are aware of this can begin the nurturing process even before the child is born.

> "A human embryo doesn't just sit, being bored, and suck its thumb. It works overtime developing a brain...three months before birth a baby's brain has more neurons than at any other time in its life...By a baby's second day of life, all of its sensory organs function soaking up information to speed to the developing brain. For the next eighteen months a baby's brain is a learning machine." (1)

According to James Shreeve (2005) on the developing child:

> "...at birth, she was already predisposed to the sound of her mother's voice over that of strangers; to the cadence of nursery rhymes she might have overheard in the womb; and perhaps to the tastes of her mother's Mexican cuisine, which she has sampled generously in the amniotic fluid. The last of her senses to develop fully was her vision. Even so, she clearly recognized her mother's face at just two days old." (2)

Psychologist, Alice Miller says in her book, *The Drama of the Gifted Child*:

> "If a woman is to give her child what he will need throughout his life, it is absolutely fundamental that

she not be separated from her newborn, for the hormones that foster and flourish her motherly instinct are released immediately after birth and continue in the following days and weeks as she grows more familiar with her baby. When a newborn is separated from his mother...then a great opportunity is missed for both mother and child.

The bonding between mother and baby after birth stimulates in both of them the feeling that they belong together, a feeling of oneness that ideally has been growing from the time of conception. The infant is given the sense of safety he needs to trust his mother... This initial mutual intimacy can never again be created, and its absence can be a serious obstacle right from the start." (3)

First 5 California is an organization with a mission to support and optimize early childhood development. They advocate for parents to: "Talk. Read. Sing" from day one:

"The moment babies come into the world, their brains are forming the connections that will determine how they learn, think, and grow. In fact, 90% of their brains are developed by age five..." (4)

Thus, during this time frame parents should be "gardening the soul" by nurturing:

• The tenderness of emotions

- The reasoning of the mind
- The loyalty of their free will
- Emotional security
- Emotional self-worth
- Emotional stability

Parent tools for nurturing: All forms of affection: cuddling, holding, hugging, kissing, talking, reading, singing.

This tool of affection may seem too simplistic or obvious. But the truth is, many parents do not know how to be affectionate. That was my experience when I first became a parent. I didn't know how to be affectionate mostly because my mother was not affectionate, and, as it turns out, neither were her parents affectionate with her. My mother once told me that she felt bad about this because she realized that she was not a very affectionate mother. She told me a story about my grandfather, who never told her he loved her or showed her any kind of affection.

One day, as she recalled, she was leaving for school in the morning. As she walked down her front steps and began walking down the street, she noticed her father walking toward her. As they got closer, she looked at him to greet him, but he just ignored her and kept on walking past her. She called out, "Papa. It's me, your daughter. Aren't you going to say hi?" But he just continued walking and ignoring her.

Unfortunately, this is not an uncommon experience for far too many children. And then we grow up and become parents and lack this vital ability to give our children what they need because we don't have it. That's the bad news. However, the good news is that being affectionate can be learned. But even if a parent struggles to be affectionate, a child can receive affection from others. Alice Miller says, "...even a mother who is not especially warmhearted can make this development possible, if she only refrains from preventing it and allows the child to acquire from other people what she herself lacks." (5)

I know this is true because I experienced it. I watched how my wife and Sicilian in-laws smothered my children with so much love and affection that it used to make me uncomfortable. I had never seen such affection...a constant and continuous attention, touching, hugging, holding, and kissing practically the whole time they were with my children especially when they were in this infant to two years old time frame. They made up for whatever affection my children were lacking from me. But I did eventually learn to be an affectionate father and remain so today and so can you! Never underestimate the powerful effect of, and need for, your physical touch, hugs, and kisses by your children.

Secret # 2: Parents are Trainers of Obedience. Time frame: two – five years old.

One of the things I enjoy doing is planting flowers and different types of vines and watching them grow to their full maturity. I like the vines that grow and crawl on fences, walls, guard rails, and wherever else I train and want them to grow.

The tricky part about potting and/or planting flowers and plants is getting them securely rooted in the right soil and sunlight. Transplanting a plant from a pod into the ground, or a bigger pot, is a delicate process and doesn't go well if you don't treat them with sensitivity. When I first started this hobby, I wasted a lot of money buying the wrong plants and discovering that they would not grow because of the temperature during the different parts of the year where I was living. But once I learned which plants did well in certain climates and learned the proper process of planting and transplanting, I knew the roots were happy and healthy because my plants flowered beautifully to full maturity.

All of this takes consistent attention, care, shaping, and pruning. And I believe the same principles apply for the healthy growth of children. The roots of their soul are vital to their full development and that is where our full attention, care, and shaping of character needs to be. It's not about controlling or dominating every aspect of your child's individuality. But just as plants will not do well without proper care of their roots, neither will children without the proper care of their character. Yet, as all parents know, this next time frame can prove to be very challenging and I find, oftentimes, too many parents give up and give in and neglect this important role, which is a big mistake.

At two years old, children are now very aware of what's happening and usually begin to challenge a parent's authority. They want what they want, when they want it, how they want it, and where they want it...now! The self and selfishness are alive and well and on full display towards both parents, siblings, and other playmates. So, now what?

Parents in this time frame, must maintain the gardener role, but add to it the role of what I call a "Trainer". Those of you who exercise regularly or belong to a physical workout program understand what I mean by having a Trainer. That person who knows you, and knows what you are trying to achieve mentally, physically, and spiritually, and is there to encourage, push, and keep you on a disciplined regimen to achieve your goals.

Obviously, a two-year-old child doesn't have these types of goals, but the same principle of needing a Trainer applies to help them develop a healthy character and sense about self, rather than allowing them to grow like a wild, unnurtured, and uncultivated plant that never grew to its potential because of unhealthy roots.

Educating the Conscience

The shaping of character is essentially a process of training the conscience. Everybody is born with a conscience. This is a natural part of our humanity: knowing the difference between right and wrong. However, having a strong obedience to, or weak response to, our conscience is an individual matter, not the same for everyone, and parents are in the best position to provide this education. Thus, as parents, when we see or hear our child unknowingly putting themselves in danger, we quickly stop them to educate them that touching a hot stove or playing too close to the street is harmful to them. When we hear them being impolite and/or saying bad words we correct them to let them know the correct and incorrect use of words. If our children disrespect our neighbors, we correct them. If they act out in school, we take responsibility and enact potential consequences to teach them proper social mores. In other words, the motivation of our parental voice of correction as their initial Trainer, educator, and voice of conscience is for the betterment of themselves in the following areas:

- Respect for self
- Respect for others
- Respect for authority
- Respect for boundaries

We know the unsettling inside our hearts when our conscience is bothering us for doing the wrong thing. We also know the calming peace and serenity gained when we have obeyed our conscience and done the right thing. Doing the right thing, and doing things right, gives us that inner peace about how we perceive ourselves, and how we treat others with dignity and respect. I suggest that these are things that parents must teach their children in the role of a Trainer.

Parent tool for Training: Consistent and proper use of discipline (Discipline will be covered in more detail in Chapter 4).

Secret # 3: Parents are Coaches on the Field of Life. Time Frame: five – twelve years old.

Our role and goal as Coaches of our children is: Preparation for separation and infiltration, not isolation. Allow me to explain.

Life is a process of separation: separation from the womb, separation from the home, separation in marriage, and eventually, separation in death. In other words, we are not raising our children to live with us for the rest of their lives. Rather, our job as parents is to prepare them to leave home one day and establish their own life, their own home, and their own family.

This is why I call this phase of parenting, *Coaching*, because at this stage of life our children are leaving home every day and playing in the game of life. They are in school for eight hours a day, five days a week, nine months a year for the next twelve years (give or take). After high school maybe they will go off to college or get a job. After that, perhaps marriage or some other venture in business, travel, or what have you.

Thus, at this point we are now like coaches, standing on the sidelines watching our children play in the game of life. We aren't in control of their every move, word, action, or choice. We are more removed from them and all that we nurtured, trained, and prepared them for will be manifested as they encounter different people in all types of different situations and circumstances.

Secondly, because of the preparation of our children, we can be confident about sending them into the community every day to *infiltrate* the darkness, the temptations, the peer pressure, the toxic environment around them, as an infiltrating light. As an example. As a leader for their peers to follow.

Many parents are afraid of the environment outside their own home, and rightfully so. They have seen how it can affect children. Too many of their own children have become casualties of their environment, with all the risky and toxic elements of drugs, alcohol abuse, gangs, violence, and other negative influences. And yet, if we live in such an environment, it can't be avoided, and trying to remove or isolate our children from the reality of our environment is not the answer either.

> "Thus, the worry of parents that violent television shows will affect their children adversely is the epitome of a chronically anxious society focusing on outside forces rather than inner strength. Parents cannot possibly hope to insulate their children from all pathogenic forces and ideas in the environment. That way of thinking has to lead to unending cycles of anxiety. Where does it end? But they can 'inoculate', so to speak, their children against those noxious forces by the maturity they instill in them through their own well-differentiated leadership. The immune response is always about self, strength, and integrity." (6)

A huge turning point in the field of medicine happened when physicians discovered that building up the human immune system was the answer to physical health, instead of working to try and rid the environment of, or isolate people from, all the toxic elements. (7) In POM I encourage parents to see themselves as the *inoculation* that builds the immune system of their child and fights off the negative toxins in their environment. This inoculation is a metaphor for building the integrity of a child, which is like your child's social immune system. Again, this is why these phases of parenting; nurturing, training, discipline, and coaching are vital to the healthiness of our children. We cannot remove these negative elements from the environment and isolating our children from them will only weaken their social immune system. As doctors discovered many years ago, a child's immune system is not fully developed at birth and the only way it can get stronger is for the child to get sick so the immune system can develop the antibodies that prohibit the sickness next time.

The parent as a coach

I enjoy coaching. I enjoy it because it is a very rewarding experience to help someone improve their performance. Their career. Their life.

Coaching is an act of service. It is servant-leadership in action because you are not the principal person performing. You are not the person the fans are coming to watch in the game. Nevertheless, you are a key person behind the scenes. You are the guide. A resource. You are the person providing the knowledge and discipline that elevates performance to a higher level. That is what coaching is all about. As I like to share about the difference between teaching and coaching: *Not all good teachers are good coaches. But all good coaches are good teachers.* What I mean by this is that good teachers have knowledge of the game and can share or explain the formations, strategies, and plays of a game. But that doesn't mean they have improved a player's game performance. That requires good coaching in addition to good teaching. Good coaching takes teaching a step further by showing the players not only the knowledge of the game, but also how to execute the strategies and plays at a superior level. By their knowledge, insights, and instruction of specific drills to practice repeatedly, they improve the players' skill level in the game, not just their knowledge of the game.

This is what parent coaching is all about. We parents are in a very influential position. Parent coaching comes with a lot of responsibility. And because you have nurtured and disciplined your children, they trust you. They listen to you. They believe in your instruction and guidance to improve their performance and achieve peak performance in the game of life.

Parent coaching tools of preparation for separation and infiltration:

- Guide your child to discover who they really are, not who their peers, rap songs, television programs, and social media say they are. Be an encourager of their personal dreams and visions.

- Encourage the development of their uniqueness. Emphasize that they are one of a kind. We are not comparing our child to him, her, or them.
- Investment of time and money for specialized knowledge and improvement of skill level.
- Be a role model by showing your children how you use your unique gifts and talents to benefit others.

In her book, *How Children Become Violent: Keeping Your Kids Out of Gangs, Terrorist Organizations, and Cults,* author Katherine Seifert, PhD. says:

Over the last three decades as a criminal justice and psychotherapist professional, I saw countless patients with either severe mental illnesses or histories of grotesquely violent behavior. As I asked them questions and delved into their pasts, it became clear that many, if not all, had experienced some level of childhood trauma in the form of neglectful, painful or violent upbringings... could there be some link between childhood trauma, and the inability to lead normal, productive lives and have empathy for others?...the majority...had histories of childhood abuse, neglect, traumatic loss of parents without sufficient substitute caregiver. (8)

By contrast, in their book, *How's Your Family Really Doing?* authors Don and Debra McMannis say:

Members of healthy families have more positive outlooks about human nature and about the possibility of changing for the better. Research by Barbara Frederickson (2001) shows that cultivating positive emotions such as gratitude and joy can help build psychological resiliency and improved emotional well-being. When people feel good about themselves, they are much more likely to share those good feelings with others.

The importance of optimizing the Home Field Advantage and understanding these three time frames as a strategic method for child development cannot be overlooked in terms of preparing children for choosing either a negative or a healthy lifestyle.

First off, I would like to thank the Kern County Sheriff's Office for letting Steve and Ryan run the (Parents on A Mission) class. Then I would like to thank Steve and Ryan for their hard work and dedication towards us inmates. They made it where I believe in myself again to do better. I now believe that coming to jail this time was a wakeup call to straighten up. I would like to be there for my children when they're growing up. My father wasn't, he's been in prison since 2008. The class has taught me how to be a better man, how to live right, how to discipline, how to think before I react, and how to make a change. Steve and Ryan have given me the courage to want to do better things in life, to have a stable family, a job, and my own things to make me happy. If it wasn't for this class, I would probably be ready to just get out and get high. I want to continue to stay clean and sober and follow up to the classes they have to offer. This class has changed my whole outlook on life. I hope I can change to do better. I just need someone to stand by me, and I know that Garden Pathways will. For that I would like to thank you two and may all of you be blessed and good luck.

– Resident, Kern County Lerdo Correctional Facility, Bakersfield, CA

4.

The Proper Use of Discipline

Before I get into the subject of discipline allow me to share three different scenarios for you to think through how you would handle each hypothetical situation. The age group I have in mind for these scenarios is elementary school age.

Scenario # 1:

You have warned your small children while eating dinner not to place their glass of milk too close to the edge of the table to avoid tipping it over and spilling or breaking the glass. While eating and having conversation, one child takes a drink of milk and places the glass at the edge of the table. Shortly thereafter, he is asked to pass the bread. As he reaches to pass the bread, he knocks over the glass, which falls to the floor, spills the milk, and breaks the glass. – What would you do? How would you handle this situation?

Scenario # 2

You gave your child specific instructions not to stay after school to play and to come straight home so you can pick them up for a dentist appointment. Upon arriving home, your child is not there. You proceed to the school and there she is playing. You ask why she did not go straight home as instructed, to which she replies, "I just forgot." You tell her she is grounded and proceed to the dentist's office. When you arrive, the receptionist tells you that your appointment was yesterday. Your child looks at you and says, "I guess you just forgot, Mom" and then wants to know if she is still grounded. – How would you handle this situation? What is your answer to your child's question?

Scenario # 3

Your child comes home from school with another of several reports of bad behavior in the classroom. You have disciplined her each time, met with the teacher and principal more than once, warned her, and done everything to try and correct the problem. – Now what would you do?

The point with these hypothetical situations is not necessarily what is the right thing to do or the wrong thing. It is more a matter of stopping to think about your response (as opposed to reacting, as we talked about in the personal growth principles in Chapter 1) given the time, place, personality of the child, and a host of other things that may have been going on before the situation came about. With that in mind, here are a few observations to consider:

- **Scenario # 1** – This scenario is to depict a "mistake". The question is, should we discipline children for mistakes? In my view, no. I suggest that mistakes provide good opportunities for a teachable moment.

  In my own personal experience with my children this was the type of thing that would cause me to react in anger, yelling, and provoking my child to tears. As a young dad I wasn't thinking about, nor did I know anything about "teachable moments," I just reacted to the fact that my child didn't listen to me and now we have a broken glass and spilled milk to clean up. Of course, as I grew in my emotional maturity, I later learned how not to react in anger to children's mistakes and use the opportunity as a teachable moment by cleaning up the mess together, to give my small children a plastic glass to drink from and remind my child why Daddy is asking them not to put their drink to close to the edge of the table.

- **Scenario # 2** – This scenario is to depict "open defiance" of authority. The question is, should we discipline children for open defiance? Answer: In my view, other than extenuating circumstances, yes, there should be consequences for open defiance regardless of the mistake of the parent.

  This is a situation where a parent needs to discern if their child really forgot or if they are simply being defiant. It is possible that a child could forget about going straight home to be ready for a dentist appointment. And in that case a parent might decide that "this time" there won't be any consequences. But if it keeps happening in other circumstances and the child continues to "forget," that is usually a matter of defiance to authority. However, in general, whether the child forgot or not, I would still enforce consequences and explain that I have consequences too for my forgetfulness; I'll need to reschedule, take another day and time off work, possibly pay a fee for not showing up, etc. I'd also add that consequences for open defiance would carry much more weight than consequences for being forgetful.

When I share these scenarios in the PUM class, this second scenario always generates the most discussion and differing opinions about whether or not there should be consequences for the child who forgot to go home as instructed.

- **Scenario # 3** – This scenario was to depict two possible situations. First, it could be a testing of will, and who's in control. The second possibility is this kind of continuing behavior can be an indicator that something deeper is bothering the child and could be a cry for help. This is why we must be sensitive and attentive to detail with each child and understand the need for discretion in dealing with an ongoing problem.

Having said that, sometimes it is simply a battle of wills and parents must ultimately win that battle!

Of the three, this is usually the most emotionally draining on parents, causing many parents to give in to the short-term battle and lose sight of the long-term effects. If this is a case of a stubborn, rebellious child refusing to behave, I offer the following long-term strategy as one solution.

First, don't be too hard on yourself. Being a good parent doesn't automatically mean our child will be obedient with us and other authority figures. The fact is, you can be a wonderful parent and your kid just continues to rebel and refuses to cooperate. Or a parent can be irresponsible and yet their kid turns out great. Those two outcomes are the exception, but it does happen. For the most part I believe if we are doing our best and continue to grow and work on our emotional maturity as suggested earlier, our stubborn, rebellious child will get it together over time.

Secondly, I encourage parents in addition to your role as a gardener, trainer, and coach, to add the role of a *farmer*.

We all know that farming is hard work and basically entails plowing, planting, watering, and cultivating, season after season. We also understand that no farmer expects a harvest overnight.

Although farming is long, hard work, the harvest will come if we persist with patience. The hope this gives parents dealing with this tough situation is knowing that the law of the harvest is on your side. Eventually, you will reap what you sow.

Here's how I break down this metaphor of the parent as a farmer:

* **Plowing = Confrontation of the heart**

   Just as plowing serves the purpose of breaking up the fallow ground to prepare it for the seed, confronting our child's wrong behavior is educating and speaking to their heart and conscience to not allow their hardheartedness to win them over in the long run. They know what they are doing is wrong. Their mind may be rationalizing their behavior, but their conscience is not in agreement with their emotions or rationalizing. Thus, by confronting their rebellious behavior we are strengthening the voice of their conscience. The importance of this "plowing the conscience" cannot be overlooked.

   Confronting our child on a consistent basis is emotionally exhausting and many parents end up losing this battle because they get worn down. It does require the courage to speak up again and again and oftentimes can turn into a heated argument. Nobody gets this right all the time (I know I didn't). It's just the nature of the situation. Nevertheless, what is important to remember is that you are coming from a place of unconditional love and want to send your rebellious child the message that you believe in them, and care about them, even though you are confronting their unacceptable behavior.

- **Planting = The seeds we plant are the words we speak**

We know words can be a powerful force for good or bad. As mentioned earlier, the old adage, *sticks and stones can break my bones, but words can never hurt me*, is probably one of the biggest misconceptions about the power of words and the effect they have on our hearts and minds. The fact is that words matter, especially the words parents use when dealing with a tough situation in the heat of the moment.

When we are upset it is very easy to say the wrong things and/or the right things in a wrong way. We can say things we don't mean. We can say things that are mean. Things that belittle, shame, and cause resentment and anger in our children. I cringe to think about all the times I have slipped into this argumentative, angry mode of dealing with rebellion, defiance, and disrespect. Nevertheless, I know what to do when that happens, as I discussed in Chapter 3 on how to earn respect for your parental authority: I admit I was wrong and apologize.

Raising a blended family of children has provided me a lot of experience with these things and I'm happy to say that I've grown throughout the years and gotten much better at practicing the principles I am sharing in this book. There are a few phrases, words I've learned to use, that help me to say a negative thing in a positive way. I encourage you to consider adopting these words (or similar ones you come up with on your own) the next time you find yourself "plowing and planting":

- *"This is not who you really are."*
- *"You're better than this."*
- *"I believe in you, but I am not going to accept this behavior from you."*
- *"I love you, but I don't love the way you are acting and treating your mother."*
- *"I'm on your side and I'm on you again because I love you and I'm trying to help you."*

- **Watering = Verbal Affirmation**

  During the farming phase of parenting, it is important to find any time, any opportunity to give verbal affirmation, compliments, and praise for good works and/or any kind of cooperation. Our rebellious child is not the enemy (though it sure does feel like it at times) and we can communicate this message by affirming good behavior for whatever reason, no matter how small a thing it might seem to be.

- **Cultivating = Affection**

  This can be hard to do during a time when you are confronting, arguing, frustrated, and emotionally burned out. Actually, I take it back…it is darn hard to do in these times.

  I can remember times when I would just let things go because I was too emotionally exhausted and didn't have it in me to be genuine in making any effort to do any of the above suggestions. I would separate myself from the room or the house and just chill out for a while and take the time I needed to regroup and catch my emotional and psychological breath. I would need to have a pep talk with myself because I knew I couldn't give in and give up the fight for winning back my child (stepchild in this particular case).

  At times I had to admit that what I was doing wasn't working and I needed to check myself and be honest about where I was being a part of the problem. I needed to read, study, and practice my personal and emotional growth principles. It was during these times that I developed different "seeds" to plant so I could expect a different harvest, and that is exactly what happened and continues to happen as of this writing.

  Author Gordon Neufeld suggests when dealing with what he calls "peer-oriented" youth that are obsessed with their phones, social media, and the internet:

Many of us despair of overcoming the competition for our children's attention posed by digital devices and the internet. This, often, is a serious and nearly intractable challenge for parents of peer-oriented youth. There really is no way out but through. We must confront the problem at the core, and we must do so patiently, diligently, and confidently....It may too late to address these digital connection issues, but it is never too late to address the underlying peer-orientation that drives it. This is a relationship matter....We should not overtly challenge a child already addicted by trying to control the behavior....attempts to control, prohibit, or deprive access will all fail in the absence of what we have called "relationship power". Better to bite our tongue, accept our sadness, and recognize and acknowledge the futility of coercive approaches that would only further embitter the parent-child relationship. (1)

If you find yourself in this "farming" role, let me encourage you here. Don't give in to your emotions and don't give up on your child. Keep plowing, planting, watering, and cultivating your own heart and that of your child. The law of the harvest is a real thing, and it is our best hope for winning back our rebellious *prodigal* son/daughter, as it were. Persist. Pray. And be patient for your harvest. Although it does not come overnight, it does come. It will come.

Dr. Neufeld continues:

> "Truly there is nothing more wounding than to feel continually rebuffed. It calls for drawing patiently and faithfully on our infinitely deep fount of unrequited love and hoping for a better day. Even if the situation leaves us feeling frustrated and hopeless, we must not abandon the field. As long as we stay open, there is a good chance that the wayward son or daughter will return." (2)

Dr. Neufeld knows of what he speaks. And so do I. I have not abandoned the field, a better day has come, and the wayward son has returned after twelve years of *farming* as described above. As of this writing, June 2023, here are the words I received written in a card on this past Father's Day:

> "Happy Father's Day! Thank you for all your love and support throughout my life. I'm glad and very thankful that our relationship has gotten better this year. May today fill you with blessings and I hope we can continue to grow our father-son relationship in a positive way."

The Controversy of Discipline

A study was done in Orange County, CA to determine which kids were causing most of the problems in the community. The study found that the kids who were re-offending were causing the majority of the problems. The re-offenders amounted to only 8% of the at-risk youth in the county. The study also discovered a common factor among re-offending kids:

> "A common denominator is that parents or guardians do not have the slightest idea where their kids go, what they are doing, and whom they are doing "it" with... parents have little, if any, positive influence on their children's behavior. The children have learned that they do not have to pay attention to what their parents say because they do not consistently enforce the rules." (3)

Many parents struggle between being:

* Too permissive
* Too strict
* Whether to spank or not

In his book, *Dare to Discipline*, the renowned child psychologist Dr. James Dobson, talks about the *"strong- willed child"* and the need for parents to learn how to *"bend the child's will without breaking their spirit"*.

I call this the skill of "Just Enough". Think of a musician who must always be fine-tuning their instrument each time they play it. With a guitar, if the musician pulls the string too hard it will break. If he does not pull it tight enough it will be out of tune. This skill of "just enough" is what a parent must learn in the use of discipline.

How to go about disciplining children to teach them respect for parental authority is controversial business these days.

Each family will have to determine what form of discipline works best for them.

Common principles for exercising discipline include:

1. Removing privileges that a child enjoys – Children learn the difference between "rights" and "privileges". Parents sometimes get these two confused or allow their children to confuse the difference between what is a right and what is a privilege.

    For example, do children have the right to: have a cell phone? Expect parents to buy them designer clothes? Have complete privacy in their bedroom? My answer to these three questions is, No. Thus, as a parent I have the right to remove or disallow these things because they are privileges—privileges I am allowing my children to have. When I remove them, I am using that as a form of discipline for one reason or another.

    Many children are under the impression that their cell phone is "theirs" and a parent has no right to take it away from them. They might even use the argument that they are "paying for it". That may be true, but that's beside the point. If my minor's phone is affecting them in negative way, a distraction from school and chores, causing sneakiness and a lack of communication at home, etc., then I, as a parent, may exercise my authority to take the phone away (however, this tactic of discipline may not be the best if the relationship is unhealthy as Dr. Neufeld alluded to in the above quote).

As another example, some children think that their room is their private property and that a parent has no right to invade their privacy. Once again, if my child's room becomes a dark, sneaky, and loud place causing disconnection from the rest of the family, a parent has every right to enter the room to find out what is going on or what is being hidden and causing the disconnection in relationship.

Of course, children do have "rights" which include the right to eat, be sheltered and clothed, and be cared for in love and safety. They have the right to speak up and seek outside help if they are being neglected or abused in any way. They have the right to an education, physical recreation, and social interaction in their neighborhoods, schools, and with friends and extended family, to name a few.

2. **Isolation through timeouts** – Isolation can be effective as a form of discipline. I think this is one of those things that works well with small children but maybe not so well with kids as they get older. If a parent chooses to use timeouts, I suggest you choose the appropriate place; sending a kid to their room might be more fun than discipline.

When I used this form of discipline when my children were little, I would take a chair and make them sit facing the wall with nothing to do, or look at, except the paint on the wall. I would say, "You sit here and think about what you did (or said). When you're ready to change your attitude and apologize let me know." It didn't take too long before I got the attitude change and apology needed.

3. **Verbal reprimand** – Scolding, reasoning, and lecturing can work if used correctly. By correctly I mean not used too often or every time we discipline our children. This was always a challenge for me because I am a teacher/coach by nature and lecturing (yelling) would just burst out of me. However, after I got older and matured as a father, I could see that lecturing and scolding was having a negative affect and causing shame and sadness in my children.

On the other hand, sometimes a scolding and/or lecture can be effective in discipline when spoken with the right degree of seriousness, sincerity, and love.

The true definition of the term "discipline"

To give us more insight and understanding about discipline let's look deeper into the root definition of the word. The term "discipline" comes from the Latin word *'disciplinare,'* which means *'to teach.'* Many people, however, associate the word with punishment, which falls short of the full meaning of the word.

Lessons from a speech given by a Major in WWI to officers in training

As I was reading a book on leadership I came across this story that I thought was a great analogy for teaching parents the difference between punishment and the purpose of discipline. In this example a military officer is training young men to assume the position of a military officer who will lead other men. He says the following:

> "You cannot treat all men alike. A punishment that would be dismissed by one man with a shrug of the shoulders is mental anguish for another. A company commander, who for a given offense has a standard punishment that applies to all, is either too indolent or too stupid to study the personalities of men...Study your men as carefully as a surgeon studies a difficult case...Remember that you apply the remedy to effect a cure, not merely to see the victim squirm."

Now let's read this statement again, except this time I'm going to substitute some of the original words to put this wise counsel in the parent-child context:

> "You cannot treat all [children] alike. A punishment that would be dismissed by one [child] with a shrug of the shoulders is mental anguish for another. A [parent], who for a given offense has a standard punishment that applies to all, is either too [lazy] or too [irresponsible] to study the personalities of [children]...Study

your [children] as carefully as a surgeon studies a difficult case...Remember that you apply the [discipline] to effect a cure, not merely to see the [child] squirm."

Two great principles for parents to apply towards using discipline:

1. Study the different personalities (temperament) of each of our children.
2. Discipline seeks to "cure". Punishment seeks revenge.

Wisdom in discipline:

- The question we must keep before us when disciplining children is: "Will my child learn and want to do better from what I'm going to do?" This of course requires emotional maturity. The capacity to stop, think, consider, and choose to respond to misbehavior, instead of reacting out of anger, is the key, albeit easier said than done.
- There are times for being firm. And there are times when mercy and understanding are called for and the wise parent knows the difference.

I liken the use of parental mercy to when an authority figure exercises discretion and decides to make an exception...to give you a break even though you are guilty as charged for a given offense. For example, have you ever been pulled over by a police officer who caught you clearly violating the law, yet for whatever reason decided to give you a pass? I have. What a relief that was! It just so happened to be my birthday when I was pulled over for speeding. After looking at my driver's license the officer said, "I see that today is your birthday." "Yes, it is," I said. "Happy birthday, Mr. Ramos, and slow down."

I think that this type of discretion by a parent from time to time is not only wise, but also goes a long way in establishing respect for your authority and a healthy acceptance of discipline in the future.

Insights from private conversations with rebellious youth

As mentioned earlier, discipline can be controversial. Many parents take offense when others like extended family, schoolteachers, coaches, counselors, psychologists, mental health experts, etc., offer their unsolicited advice and opinions about how parents are disciplining their children. And even though it's all well intended, parents have a hard time hearing a message that is basically telling them they need to do a better job in disciplining their children. The voice, however, that is often missing from giving parents feedback on their disciplinary ways is from those on the receiving end of the discipline: children.

As a school counselor I had the unique opportunity to hear and listen to that voice. Here are some of the common themes I heard:

- We never discuss anything after we have a confrontation.

- Many troubled youths believe their parents love their younger or "good" siblings more.
- Too many get the message they are no longer wanted at home or valued as an important member of the family.
- Many felt their parents were guilty of making bad choices in how they handled the wrong behavior of their children but would not admit it.

What I discovered from these conversation (and later conversations with the parents of my students) was how misunderstanding through miscommunication is at the root of most broken child-parent relationships. And one of the things so prevalent today that is destroying communication between children and their parents is smart phones and social media. I will address this issue in more depth in Chapter seven. For now, suffice it to say that part of our disciplining of our children must include communication that we initiate. We shouldn't allow our children to interpret our actions and decisions of how and why we used the discipline we chose in a given situation. They usually have a completely different take on a disciplinary situation. A good practice (once things have calmed down) is to discuss with your child why you chose to discipline them, listen to their feedback, and if necessary, apologize. And always bring closure with an affirming hug and words of love and encouragement.

Discipline and the word "No"

The following are two common errors I believe many parents overlook. And, as far as I know, other parent curriculums do not touch on the following two particular important child-rearing principles. (4)

Unfortunately, there can be greater consequences for children who never learn to accept that little word, *no*, from their parents. After all, what really is the difference between youth out late beyond their curfew, and at greater risk for danger, and those who have come home on time, or did not go out at all? Often the only difference was obedience to the word of parental authority that said, "No, you can't stay out longer," or "No, you can't go out."

Parents can avoid many negative ramifications by teaching their children to respect, accept, and obey the answer "No." How many teens have suffered consequences they now regret simply because they refused to accept the authority of a parent who said "No"?

The two biggest mistakes parents of young children can make:

- Not teaching small children to accept "No" for an answer.
- Not teaching small children to accept the "No" answer without an attitude.

While some parents do teach their children to accept their "No" answer, what they don't do is follow up and deal with the ugly attitude that comes along with accepting the *no* answer. In my view, overlooking this attitude is a big mistake. I strongly suggest this is a battle that must be won by correct, consistent, fair, and firm discipline.

Mother Wesley

Susanna Wesley (January 1699 – July 1742) was widely known and respected for her child-rearing principles. She was the 25th of 25 children and she and her husband had 19 of their own children. Thus she learned a thing or two about child-rearing, even though nine of her children died as infants and at her death only eight of her children were still alive. (5) Nevertheless, despite the sad loss of several of her children, Mother Wesley (as she was known) remained a model of healthy and successful child-rearing. Two of her sons, John, and Charles Wesley, were famously known for their evangelistic efforts and were founders of the Methodist Church denomination. Toward the end of her life, her son, John Wesley, asked her to write down her child-rearing principles for him and other parents he felt could benefit from them. Here is one excerpt on the importance of discipline with small children:

> "In order to form the minds of children, the first thing to be done is to conquer the will and bring them into an obedient temper. To inform the understanding is a work of time, and must with children proceed by slow degrees as they are able to bear it; but the subjecting of the will is a thing that must be done at once, and the sooner the better...For by neglecting timely

correction, they will contract a stubbornness and obstinacy which is hardly ever after conquered....In the esteem of the world, those who would withhold timely correction would pass for kind and indulgent parents, whom I call cruel parents, who permit their children to get habits they know must afterwards be broken. Nay, some are so stupidly fond as in sport to teach their children to do things which in the after while, they must severely beat them for doing."

Of course, we don't advocate "beating" children (I think what Mother Wesley meant by "beat" was spanking, which I will address shortly) but this language is not surprising coming from a mother in 18ᵗʰ century England. Nevertheless, my point is, when parents neglect to deal with the inner attitude of defiance and disrespect for the authority of parents, it is along the same lines as where Mother Wesley says, *"for by neglecting timely correction, they will contract a stubbornness and obstinacy which is hardly ever after conquered."*

This reminds me of the story of the father who was trying to control the disorderly and distracting behavior of his child at church, who refused to be quiet and sit down during the service. After trying to verbally control his child to no avail, the father finally threatened to take his son outside for a spanking if he did not behave. At that, the little boy finally obeyed and sat down. After sitting down, the boy looked at his father defiantly and said, "I might be sitting down on the outside, but on the inside, I am still standing up!"

This what I'm referring to as a big mistake many parents make by allowing their children to outwardly obey, but neglect to deal with the inner attitude of their reluctant obedience. Outward conformity is not inward respect and obedience. And as disobedient children grow old enough and big enough, our threats and bribes no longer work and they disrespect, defy, and disobey our parental authority. When parents allow, overlook, and ignore this inner defiance of their child, they often end up rewarding it and reinforcing this attitude.

Here's an illustration: A defiant child asks for permission to do something, but his parent says "No" and then asks the child to do some house chores instead. The child obeys, but has a bad attitude, making life miserable for everyone else in the house, especially younger siblings. The child angrily slams doors while doing chores, is throwing things around, giving half an effort, and has a long face and short angry answers for others in the house. The parent warns the child several times, but the parent is getting the *outward obedience* and decides to leave the attitude alone. The following day Aunt Maria calls and offers to take the kids to the mall and out to eat. But the mother decides that the child giving everyone a bad time with her attitude will not be allowed to go with Aunt Maria. Now the child is begging to go and reminding the reluctant parent that they "obeyed". "I did what you told me to do yesterday," they say, and the mother, wanting to be on good terms again, reasons in her mind, "Well, she did do what I asked," and gives permission to go.

This is a common occurrence as most parents know (I must admit I've been guilty of this myself). Emotionally worn down, we just want some peace and quiet and sometimes take the easy road by giving in to the pressure of letting our kids off the hook too easily.

Why does this matter? What is wrong with this picture?

- The parent has rewarded the inner, defiant attitude.
- The parent missed the opportunity to give the proper consequences for the inner attitude.
- The parent also demonstrated to younger siblings that as long as they outwardly obey, they will still get to do the fun things they want to do

Key Point

Children must be brought into a healthy understanding that outward conformity with an inner attitude of defiance is unacceptable and that consequences are still in force until the inner attitude is transformed into a sincere apology and a rightful respect for authority. Parents will not gain the respect and inward obedience they seek unless they are consistent in bringing consequences for:

- Wrong behavior.
- A wrong attitude for the consequences of the wrong behavior.

Here are some additional insights regarding discipline:

1. The concept that love results from the satisfying of personal desire is a deception. If parents allow themselves to be deluded by this deception, they will produce self-centered young adults. Parents who provide strict controls over their children's insatiable and self-centered natures are the parents who will eventually receive true appreciation and love from their children. Conversely, parents who give their children everything they want eventually receive the rejection and hatred they sought to avoid by trying to buy love. Counselors who work with runaway youth have isolated a consistent attitude in many of these youths. They have found that these youths usually believe their parents did not love them because the parents would neither restrain nor direct them. They felt rejected because their parents did not care enough about them to protect them from themselves. These parents rejected their parental responsibility, and thereby the youths felt rejected. Delinquent parents produce delinquent youth. A child inherently equates parental pressure with parental love...Children know they are loved and accepted by parents who care enough to use the necessary pressure to control them. The following article illustrates this point:

   Dear Ann Landers: Every now and then some teenager complains about his folks treating him as if he was still in [diapers]. He resents being asked, 'Where

are you going?' 'Who with?' 'When will you be back?'
Well, my folks never ask me any of those questions.
I am free to come and go as I please, and I don't like
it much. I have the feeling if they really cared about
me, they would make some rules. But when rules
are made, somebody has to enforce them—and that
means work. It's easier to let kids run wild. How I wish
my mother would say, 'No, you can't go ice-skating
with that clod.' But she never would. She always says,
'It's up to you.' I feel frightened and alone because I
have too many decisions to make. I hope those kids
whose parents ask a lot of questions and do a lot of
bossing know how lucky they are. It means somebody
loves them. On my own in Bridgeport, CT. (6)

2. The parent who grants privileges or enforces rules er-
ratically invites rebelliousness by unwittingly establishing freedoms for the child. The parent who only
sometimes prohibits between-meal sweets may create for the child the freedom to have such snacks. At
that point, enforcing the rule becomes a much more
difficult and explosive matter because the child is no
longer merely lacking a never-possessed right but is
losing an established one...We should not be surprised then, when research shows that parents who
enforce discipline inconsistently produce generally
rebellious children." (7)

3. Bad Brain Habits: In general, I have found another dis-
turbing trend over the past twenty-five years. Parents

are giving in more and more to difficult behavior. If a child has a habit of whining and crying to get his or her way and the parents give in to such behavior, they have taught the child's brain to whine and cry, making him more vulnerable to mood and emotional problems later on. The two words I like best in effective parenting are *firm* and *kind*. Children need love, attention, and affection, but they also need rules and discipline for their brain to develop properly.

Another way to develop a bad brain habit with children is by allowing them to endlessly argue with parents. When you allow children to chronically oppose or argue with you, you actually encourage their brain to be less flexible. When the brain area called the anterior cingulate gyrus works too hard...people get stuck on negative or oppositional thoughts and behaviors...Stopping argumentative behavior actually helps the brain work better. One of the best ways to do this is to directly deal with the behavior. On the bulletin board in our five-year-old's room is a set of seven family rules. One of the rules is "No arguing with parents. As your parents, we want to hear your opinion. More than twice constitutes arguing." This way, arguing is the exception, and cooperation is encouraged. If Chole argues, there is a consequence. When she cooperates, there are smiles and rewards. (8)

The BIG "S" Question – What About Spanking?

"French parliament recently passed new legislation that now deems spanking children to be a civil offense…the French parliament passed the Equality and Citizenship Bill, which bans all forms of corporal punishment, including spanking, caning and flogging. "The adoption of this new legislation marks a very important commitment towards the protection from violence of more than 14 million children living in France," says S.R.S.G. Santos Pais, commending the parliament for passing the bill. "Ending cruel, degrading or humiliating treatment is an indispensable component of a comprehensive national strategy for the prevention and elimination of violence against children. It lays the foundation for a culture of respect for children's rights; safeguards children's dignity and physical integrity; and encourages positive discipline and education of children through non-violent means." (9)

This issue is very controversial and one I believe deserves to be addressed and discussed in a fair and honest manner. To characterize spanking as a form of violence just isn't accurate. I can agree that "caning" and "flogging" are inappropriate forms of child discipline. But to put "spanking" in that same category is a misrepresentation of how many parents use spanking as a form of discipline. It is true that some parents' practice of "the rod of correction" can go overboard and become abusive. We all understand that. However, to paint all parents who spank their children with the broad brush of committing acts of violence and degrading their children is unfair and simply wrong. This is exactly why this issue needs to be discussed in a civil, open-minded manner.

"Spanking" needs to be properly defined. Spanking is not a beating, slapping, punching, kicking, or any other form of physically hurting a child. A spanking is painful. I'll give you that. But it should never be physically abusive and does not need to be psychologically harmful either.

Therapists, psychologists, family counselors, and others will point to a plethora of "research" and "studies" to justify their opinions and lend credibility to their argument against spanking. But we have all been subjected to research and studies that are false, inaccurate, and biased. (10) What these advocates who support taking away parental authority want is for people like me, that work with parents, youth, and families, to tell parents that they should not spank their children for any reason because it is an act of violence that can cause mental and psychological problems in children later in life.

First of all, I do not believe it is an act of violence. Secondly, it is not my place to take away the right of parents to use *proper* spanking as a form of discipline should they choose to do so. Thirdly, I believe when spanking is used properly it can be effective as a form of discipline for some children (I will address what POM considers proper spanking below). But none of those reasons are my primary purpose for addressing this topic.

My purpose is to keep a promise—a promise I made to the students on my caseload many years ago when I was the at-risk counselor on a school campus.

At that time (the early 1990s) I told my students that if they would be honest with me and tell me what was really bothering them and why they were basically destroying their future by the risks and dangerous lifestyle choices they were making, that I would stand up for them. I promised I would come alongside them and speak for them to the school principal, police, or their parents. This prompted them to open up to me about what was going on behind closed doors. And that prompted me to begin to do home visits. As a young parent myself at that time, I knew better than to believe everything a young teen was telling me. I knew that there are always two sides to the story.

To be clear, I'm not saying all of them accused their parents of abuse of one kind or another. But some did and that was something I could not ignore, legally or emotionally. As I shared earlier on how POM was started, this was one of my primary motivations, as well as the lack of communication, respect, relationship, and overall dysfunction I witnessed during my home visits.

One of the things I discovered was how many parents confuse spanking and/or discipline with physical abuse, and that many parents justify physical abuse in the name of spanking and discipline.

It amazes me how many youth advocates know that children are being improperly "spanked" and disciplined, yet they refuse to address it. They would rather just criminalize parents by calling Child Protective Services without discussing these issues first and making the effort to educate parents that are good people, mean well, and are often just following the discipline practices that they were raised with. Don't get me wrong. Obviously if real physical abuse is taking place and continues to take place, then by all means the authorities must be called upon to remove a child from such ongoing abuse. That said, in many cases if parents can be confronted in a spirit of care and empathy, this situation can be corrected without threatening to take away parents' authority and worse, their children.

For example, one parent told me after completing the POM classes, *"I never knew it was wrong to slap my kids. After taking the classes I realized how this was wrong and affecting my relationship with them."*

Thus, the POM curriculum does not shy away from this issue, nor take the easy road of criminalizing and disempowering parents who spank or shaming them into believing they are terrible and irresponsible people. Frankly, given the gravity of this issue, I think that is a cowardly way of handling this issue. Shaming and criminalizing parents who spank children, and disempowering parental authority from those who are ignorantly disciplining their children is an easy, wrong, and irresponsible non-answer to correct the problem.

To be clear, POM does not advocate spanking, nor make an argument for the right or wrong about spanking. The important point is: Whether we agree with it or not, or like it or not, many parents do in fact spank their children, and that's why we should address it.

In our POM classes we openly talk about spanking and make the effort to educate parents who spank to strike a wise balance by suggesting several principles for those parents who choose spanking as a form of discipline.

This is my way of keeping my promise. I refuse to remain silent and not speak up for and defend all the physically abused children who have no voice. We can threaten parents and try to legislate this issue away, but it hasn't and won't correct the problem. My experience, after working with and building a trusting relationship with parents, has been to witness a change of heart and adjustment in disciplinary practices.

The POM curriculum addresses the topic of spanking by offering some guidelines and suggested principles:

- POM does not make an argument for right or wrong on the practice of spanking.
- If parents exercise their right to spank, they should do it properly, but we should not assume that they are doing it properly, which is why we should discuss it.
- We can't expect parents who choose to spank to stop just because others are against it.

- Many parents do not agree with spanking children for any reason. Many other parents do in fact spank their children. Whether we are for it, or against it, both views must be respected.
- Many parents are under the false assumption that it is illegal to spank children. But it is not illegal. (11) However, there are certain limitations and these need to be clarified.
- What *is* illegal is physically abusing children. Guidance is needed for those parents who do spank to ensure they understand what abuse is and practice discipline through spanking properly.

Suggested guidelines: If you choose to spank, be wise and moderate.

1. POM suggests spanking be used as a last resort.
2. Parents should not wait until they are angry before spanking.
3. Parents should explain what behavior the child is being spanked for.
4. Using the hand for one or two swats on the posterior only is sufficient.
5. Parents should talk about the behavior later to bring understanding, reconciliation, and closure.
6. *Slapping, punching, kicking, beating and any other form of physical force that is physically harmful to the child is abuse and never acceptable.*
7. What is proper spanking? A spank on the posterior— nothing more, nothing less.

8. When should the use of spanking stop? In general, once a child reaches the age of twelve, other forms of discipline are better suited that recognize the growth and maturity of the child who is beyond the spanking stage. (The age of twelve is only a suggested guideline. Each parent can decide for themselves.)

In the spirit of full disclosure and transparency, I leave you with this thought. I did spank my children as a form of discipline. However, the reason I spanked my children was so I wouldn't need to spank them thereafter. It worked.

References for further study:

https://www.ctvnews.ca/contentious-study-says-spanking-may-benefit-children-1.471361

https://srcd.onlinelibrary.wiley.com/doi/10.1111/cdev.13701
https://www.psychologytoday.com/us/blog/the-age-overindulgence/202211/does-any-good-come-spanking-children

What did you think about the POM Experience?

Very good! This class is very needed in all communities. I believe this should be taught to parents as a mandatory for birthing. This is the 'instruction book' we have all been waiting for. Thank you!! – Staff member, Colorado Department of Corrections

I was very skeptical about this training. I was hopeful for something that would be good for our guys and not another parenting curriculum filled with stats and psychological theories. I was not disappointed. This material, this theory, is more than I could have hoped for. This training was fantastic. There are so many things that I can use in my own personal family. I am going to change the obedience with an attitude at my house. I am going to ask for forgiveness from my family for being so crazy sometimes. I think that this will be great for our guys as well.
– Staff member, Colorado Department of Corrections

This course caused me to look at myself and re-evaluate how I do things and think. Even though my children are grown, I can implement these principles in their lives and help them implement them in their children's lives when they have children. I look forward to presenting this to any and all that will listen.
– Staff member, Colorado Department of Corrections

5.

Building Safe Communities

"History clearly affirms that family is the foundation of society. It is the building block of all civilizations. It is the glue by which everything is held together."
– Anonymous

THE LIMA BEAN STORY

Our story begins with a young boy and girl, brother and sister, and their aging grandparents. Both the grandmother and grandfather are very old and respected elders of the tribe from the far-away land where they were born. Old Grandmother and Old Grandfather are very sad that the children's world in this new country has lost the spirit of community that the grandparents always knew among the people of their own birth village. So they never miss an opportunity to teach and remind the young children of the ancient ways and traditions of their ancestors.

Today, the four of them are sitting together in the soft grass under a great ancient oak tree. Old Grandmother has brought along a crumpled paper bag filled with dried lima beans, "My precious little ones, let me show you the people of my village," she says to the curious brother and sister, as she slowly lays out the dried beans one by one in a circle on the carpet of grass. As she creates this circle, with each carefully placed bean Old Grandfather begins to describe the person in the village each one represents. "Now here is the man who bakes such good bread for us. And this one is our neighbor who brought food to your mother when she was too sick to work.

And over here is the funny lady down the street who makes us laugh. This one here is the old man who lives down by the river, the one who, in his sadness, drinks too many strong spirits."

And so Old Grandmother and Old Grandfather continue around the circle of beans, representing many different people—all kinds of people—to make up the village, the community. When the circle is complete, Old Grandfather turns to the young boy and girl and says, "Now it's your turn. You may choose any of the people the two of you wish from our village to make a community of your own. Who will you choose, I wonder?" As the grandparents watch, the little boy and girl select the dried beans carefully, one by one to form another circle next to the first circle—a community of their own making. When they were finished, three beans were left from Old Grandmother's original circle. She turns and says, "Let's see who you did not choose to be in your village. Tell us who the three are." "This one is the old drunk man who lives down by the river. He's dirty and he smells awfully bad! says the young girl. "That's true," says Old Grandmother, "He doesn't have a warm house to live in with a nice bath like you do. Of course, if he lived in a house instead of on the riverbank, he never would have been where he needed to be to save the life of the boy who wandered away from home and fell into the water. That child surely would have drowned! Do you remember? So then the little boy, Reginald, would not be in your village either. This bean would have to be taken out of your village too." Old Grandmother removes another bean from the circle, while the young girl moves uncomfortably on the grass.

"Now who is this?" asks Old Grandfather, pointing to the second rejected bean. The young boy answers, "That's the crazy lady whose little girl was killed in the car accident. She sings to herself and talks funny. I'm afraid of her!" "She is very strange," Old Grandfather agrees. "Let's leave her out, too. But you must remember that now you will miss the beautiful music she makes with her guitar, because she won't be here to play for us any longer." Old Grandfather removes another bean, and the young boy looks disappointed, but says nothing. "And this one?" asks Old Grandmother, pointing to the last bean. "This one is the man who had a gun and went to jail," says the young girl. "He's very bad," says the young boy. "Oh, yes, I know him," says Old Grandmother, "He's the one who always sends money to his mother, brothers and sisters. Did you know he made his little brother go back to school instead of selling drugs in the streets?" Old Grandfather reached toward the circle of beans and says, "I think you'd better take this whole family out of your village now, because without this man they would have to move away and find another place to live. Some of them might even be in jail themselves without this man. We have to take all their beans out. How many? Let's see: seven. None of them will be in your village now." The young boy's face falls, and the young girl has a tear in her eye, as the seven beans are removed from the circle. Both of them are silent for a while. After a few moments, the young girl says, "It will be very hard to live with some of these people in our village, but I guess we need them all." The young boy agrees, "They all belong, don't they? Just like us." And Old Grandmother and Old Grandfather lean back against the great, ancient oak tree, and smile. (1)

Points of community building from the story:

- **Extended family can be a powerful resource for teaching youth the value of all people in the community.** This is a great example and inspiration for us grandparents in the role we can have in teaching our grandchildren. This is a little harder in our mobile society where families don't seem to live in the same close vicinity like when I was growing up. Yet there still are many opportunities to be influential in our grandchildren's lives during holiday visits and using the internet and social media platforms available to help us stay connected.
- **The brother and sister learned together.** Home is the proper place to teach children how to build healthy

relationships, which start in the home and then carry over into the community. I do believe that families that learn together, play together, work together, and pray together, stay together. Of course, as children grow older, they will discover their own journey and develop their own purpose, but they will still have an appreciation for the value of community and pass it on to their children someday, just like the grandparents did in the story.

- **Healthy communities don't prejudge their members.** Children model their behavior on what they see and hear from their parents. Children are also innocent and not expected to always embrace other things and people they are not familiar with. Thus, as we saw in the story, the boy and the girl showed prejudice towards the individuals in their grandparents' community that they did not know personally, and were simply judging them from a shallow and ignorant frame of reference. This is one of the major points of the story and a lesson we desperately need taught and modeled by parents in our homes today.

It is interesting to note who the children rejected from their community: 1) The old drunk man; 2) The crazy lady whose child was killed; 3) The man who had a gun and went to jail. On the surface it might seem normal, easy even, for a child to dismiss and reject a drunk, a crazy person, and an incarcerated person. But what's worse is when adults reject and ostracize such people without compassion or empathy for reasons why or how some people end up in less than favorable situations. Thank God for the grandparents of these two children. Their example in this wise story is what our current generation needs more of today as we witness much of the same prejudice and ignorance in present-day society that has lost the "spirt of community".

- **Knowing family and community history helps connect children with their community.** Do our children know the true history of their family, community, and country? If so, or if not, why is this important? It is important because of the need to belong. The need to take pride in something bigger that self. The need to choose loyalty to and pledge our allegiance to family, community, country.

  Without the knowledge of history, we have nothing to anchor ourselves in. We are lacking the larger purpose of commitment. We lose the meaning of our existence. We are absent of the "Why?"

  > The ability to attract so many people from across the country, of all colors and races, to join together on the right day, at the right time, took something special. Though others knew what had to change in America to bring about civil rights for all, it was Martin Luther King who was able to inspire a country to change not just for the good of the minority, but for the good of everyone. Martin Luther King started with Why. (2)

Once the grandparents were able to enlighten the children about the history of the individuals they had rejected, they understood *Why* these people mattered and *Why* their contribution to the community was important and needed. The *Why* from their history caused a paradigm shift in the children, immediately followed by a change in attitude and behavior towards the people they knew nothing about before they rejected them.

- **Children must be taught the value of community unity in diversity.** If there was ever a time in our society for parents to talk with and teach their children the value of *healthy* diversity and inclusion vs. a cancel culture, now is that time.

I grew up in what were considered the radical sixties and seventies, the counterculture revolution, the protest songs, the protest of the Vietnam War, the drug culture, the hippie culture, free love, the feminist movement, flower children, Woodstock, and the civil rights movement and riots.

What we have today has certainly built upon the counterculture, but in my view with much more emphasis on diversity. Diversity of family types, sexual and gender orientation, and educational-social mores are under intense rearrangement in today's America. Be these things as they may, I believe there can be value in diversity, value in dissent, and value in disagreement.

But that value will not be understood or enjoyed now or in years to come if parents are not having open conversations about these things and teaching that *all* human beings deserve respect regardless of whether we agree with their lifestyle choices or not. It's okay to disagree, but we must learn and teach how to disagree in an agreeable manner. That is not what we see today, especially as demonstrated by our universities, public schools, mainstream media, corporations, and elected leaders in government.

Today it's not so much about the counterculture as it is about the cancel culture: canceling disagreement, dissent, and diversity of opinions not in alignment with certain ideologies favored by people in power. That is not the spirit of community we need and definitely does not express the value of diversity that the powers that be claim to represent. Therefore, in POM we admonish parents that they are the key to safe neighborhoods. They are the most important persons in the community when it comes to raising a generation of citizens who can build and keep the spirit of true inclusivity, which fosters honest and healthy community unity in a diversity of cultures, ethnicities, and opinions.

Community building in the home

Community building in the home begins by developing relationships in the home that foster appreciation, respect, caring, and fun with family members first. Family interactions provided on a regular, daily basis can be used to teach children the importance of:

Dependence – Small children receive security and a sense of self-worth as their daily needs are tended to by parents. They also need instruction to learn to appreciate the dependence they have on parents to meet their needs. While it is normal for small children to be attended to by their parents, we should also be attentive to any development of an attitude of entitlement or demanding of parents and/or taking our services to them for granted.

Independence In addition, as our children get a little older, they need to be taught the importance of being able to fend for themselves as an individual expected to be responsible for their own needs that serves to develop a healthy work ethic that will translate to citizenship that makes a positive contribution to the larger community.

As an example, when your child says, "Mom, I'm hungry." You respond by saying, "Well, there's some leftovers in the refrigerator you can warm up for yourself." Or, "Mom, all my clothes are dirty." To which you reply, "Okay, let me show you how to use the washing machine to wash them." You get the idea. Now, is this being a mean or lazy parent? No. We are simply teaching our children to be responsible and tend to their own needs at a level that is very doable for their age.

Interdependence – There needs to be a cultivation of the humility to accept how we need each other to complete the fullness of our life. This is usually a slow process that takes time away from the normal day-to-day home life they have experienced in their early stages of life. As our children grow into the teenage years and beyond, they need some space to discover and grow into their individuality. They want more independence. This is common to all teens and young adults. However, as they get out of the house and explore the world, so to speak, eventually they discover that they still need their parents. They still need their siblings, extended family, and close friends. In other words, they develop an appreciation for the value of interdependence.

I suggest that this time cycle of moving from dependence to independence and then to interdependence, first learned in the home, is a microcosm of the macro community. As citizens we are dependent upon the functions and provisions expected from the four basic institutions of communities: government, business, education, and religion. At the same time, as individuals, we are independent employees and entrepreneurs providing for ourselves and our families. And finally, as individual families we realize we are interdependent on each other, which makes up the larger community.

Children learn to appreciate and develop family "community" at home because of parents who:

1. **Plan and prioritize a consistent daily schedule.** Eat dinner together without TV, phone calls, texting, or email

interruptions. Many families eat dinner together but still allow these distractions that disrupt good conversation that builds family unity and community. Having a set time for dinner might not seem like a big deal, but it is. In his book, *Our Kids: The American Dream in Crisis*, author Robert D. Putnam refers to a study by child development specialist Jane Waldfogel. (3)

> "Waldfogel has shown that…family dining is a powerful predictor of how children will fare as they develop. 'Youths who ate dinner with their parents at least five times a week…did better across a range of outcomes: they were less likely to smoke, to drink, to have used marijuana, to have been in a serious fight, to have sex…or to have been suspended from school, and they had higher grade point averages and were more likely to say they planned to go to college. ' " (4)

Having dinner together is not a time for texting, social media, or anything else that distracts children from having a healthy dialogue and eye-to-eye contact with father and mother. I'm not saying that family dinners are a guarantee or the magic solution to winning the loyalty of our children. However, what I am saying is that parents who plan family dining are making a wise investment and creating an experience for their children that will go a long way in winning the battle for loyalty. I can attest to this based on my own personal experience.

As my children were growing up, family dinners were a ritual in our home and the connection we created during those times remain strong to this day. Back in those days my kids were not distracted with smart phones, texting, social media and the like. Yet, the TV, music, and the house phone ringing were all potential distractions that I did not allow to interrupt our dinner time. We talked, we laughed, we enjoyed each other's company. Another thing that I did to protect our dinner time was to not allow friends at our dinner table. I know that sounds harsh but that leads me to my next suggestion where I'll explain.

2. **Plan and organize fun family activities**. These activities can be simple games played at home, outings to the park or beach, simply going to a movie together as a family (Something that most families enjoy at home now with all the different streaming options), or a yearly family vacation. Again, these are special times for building connection and attachments for a lifetime. For that reason, I suggest parents should use discretion in allowing friends or even extended family members to join them because when friends or extended family members are present it often changes the family relational dynamics. Keeping these special times to "just us" allows genuine conversation, family camaraderie, sibling friendships to deepen, and family traditions and memories to be established.

I'm sure we have all seen how Mom or Dad *change* when company comes to the house. Suddenly Dad, who normally has little to say when he comes home from work, becomes the life of the party talking, joking, laughing. Then the kids wonder and think to themselves: "Gee, Dad, why can't you act like that when it's just us?" Or the reverse might be true. Mom, who normally is the light and life at home talking, laughing, and/or singing, becomes a different person when the in-laws or other adult friends come over. The same changes in personality happen with the kids as well. Older brother starts yelling at or talking down at little sister or embarrassing his younger brother wanting to show-off to his friends. Little sister wants to hang out with her older sister and her friends but is pushed away, which is unusual behavior for her older "best friend" sister. Another thing I've noticed is that cousins or friends start forming little cliques that leave others out and cause hurt and jealousy.

You might say that these things are just natural occurrences and are nothing to worry about. Maybe. Maybe not. But why rob your children of those special times with "just us"? Why not cultivate a safe environment where we can all get to know each other on a deeper level and not have to worry about putting up a front to impress others outside our immediate family.

Don't misunderstand me. Over the course of time, there were many nights when I did allow or invite my children's friends to have dinner with us. And we had many great times on special outings, parties, and dinners with extended family. I'm not advocating that "others" should *never* join our family for dinner or vacation. That's taking it too far and not healthy for our children. Nevertheless, it's important for parents to be aware of and know how to balance "just us" times with fun activities that include others in developing an atmosphere of freedom, acceptance, joy, affection, and unconditional love.

I understand families have different time commitments that makes it seem almost impossible to plan and set aside time for these special activities. The craziness of work, commuting to and from work and school, homework, meetings at school, church, weekend sports, birthday parties, and other special events, cause us to move too fast to slow down and just enjoy each other with no agenda, place to be, or people to deal with.

One of the yearly "just us" times we enjoyed was a vacation to Big Bear (a popular mountain ski resort in California) during the Christmas break. We had so much fun together doing different things that we didn't normally do at home. For example, there is no snow in Santa Barbara and therefore no opportunity to bobsled down the hills full of snow like there is in Big Bear. Another highlight of our vacation was playing games together, especially when it came to playing Monopoly. But you don't have to go on vacation or drive to a mountain resort. There are plenty of opportunities right in the city or town where you live—opportunities to build "just us" time right in your own backyard...right in your own home. Try it and see what happens.

3. **Insist on a commitment to each other's important activities** – Each family member should attend (unless legitimate circumstances don't allow) and support each parent's and/or sibling's significant activity such as school plays, sporting events, awards ceremonies, etc.

My three daughters grew up on the baseball diamond, basketball court, and football fields watching their two older brothers compete. When they grew and joined their own athletic competition in cheerleading, ballet, and basketball, my boys weren't always keen on going to watch their special "girl" events. But I didn't allow that and made them go. I'd say, "Your sisters attended your games (they didn't have a choice, of course) and now it's your turn to support them."

A lot of parents don't do that. And even more sadly, a lot of parents can't do that because their children have lost respect for their authority (I addressed this in Chapter Two) and their children are dictating what they will and won't do and where they will and won't go. Why does this matter? It matters because we are building community. We are teaching the value of support and concern for others that are values integral to a healthy community.

4. **Monitor the daily dialogue between all family members** – We need to have an ear for how our children address each other. There is always room for nicknames and joking with each other in a loving way. I'm not talking about that. I'm talking about unkind words, name-calling, and being mean to one another with words. Children listen to and pick up words from everyone and everywhere. If we are paying attention to the lyrics in the music they listen to, the dialogue on social media, the movies we watch, and the language some parents use around other adults, it should come as no surprise when we hear our children parroting these same profane words with each other. The point is, what are we going to do about it? Or is this just another case where we look the other way and not worry about it? "It's just part of growing up...isn't it?" I suppose it is. Yet, I still believe parents can provide proper coaching to instill the values of etiquette, politeness, courtesy, and respect for how we speak to one another, beginning in our home.

I understand that when our kids get older, and when they are not at home, they are going to do and say things we might not approve of at home. After all, I did the same thing—one manner of talking at home, another way of speaking to friends and in the streets.

But what we are talking about here is building citizenship. Building community in the home that will carry forward into the public square. I believe our neighbors, teachers, police, businesses, and employers appreciate young people who present themselves with what back in the day used to be called "having manners".

One way to do this is to play games together. This allows parents to build sportsmanship and also monitor language used between siblings, correct for disrespectful language and teach how to apologize, and ask for and receive forgiveness if their competitive nature crosses the line of inappropriate behavior.

5. **Develop family traditions** – For example: attending church together, yearly camping, holiday, dinners, etc. As mentioned earlier, I was not raised with any family traditions, so I created my own. I'm suggesting something with you and your children that becomes a yearly "thing" that everyone looks forward to that carries into their adult years, hopefully something they will carry on long after we parents are gone. Usually, these kinds of traditions can be built around the holidays. That's what we did with our children as they were growing up. But with a little creativity there are many ways to develop family traditions that become another form of attachment and building family unity and community.

6. Volunteer for community service together – There are ample opportunities for volunteer service in every community via schools, churches, nonprofit organizations, and the like. Intentionally involving your children in community service in one form or another creates a sense of caring, belonging, and allegiance to things that are bigger than ourselves, which is an important and mature attitude children need to learn from parents as the way good citizens give to and build safe and healthy communities.

Tips for raising good citizens who contribute to safe communities

Below are five principles I encourage parents to use as guidelines for teaching children citizenship and community contribution:

1. **Teach children:**
   - Their life is not an accident.
   - They were born on purpose, with a purpose.
   - They exist for a reason bigger than just themselves.
   - They have a significant role to play in the community.
   - Success and significance are found in service to others. (Use movies, stories, books, friends, relatives, etc., to find examples of people who used their gifts and talents to make great contributions to their community.)

2. **Tell children:**
   - Their life is a reward and a blessing, not a burden.
   - Through letters how you feel about them. Send them a card in the mail to acknowledge positive contributions they make to the family, school, or community. When appropriate, ask older siblings or extended family members to do the same.

3. **Help children:**
   - Discover their gifts and talents.
   - Get involved in sports, arts, music, and other activities that will bring out their natural talents.
   - Be who they are. Hide any disappointment you may feel if your son is not the "star athlete" or your daughter is not the "star dancer" you hoped they would be. Be sensitive to the unique development of each individual child. Nobody forms well in someone else's mold.
   - Partner with schools and be encouraged to question school officials, school policies, curriculum subjects, or other aspects of your child's education.

4. **Develop children:**
   - Invest and expose them to mentors who have accomplished their dreams.
   - Coach them to practice and appreciate discipline that sharpens skill.
   - Participate in community events with your kids to show them how others are using the same talents they have to make a difference.

5. **Prepare your children:**
   - For their destiny in society and the world.
   - Use television programs, commercials, news, movies, and music to teach your children how to analyze, think, and learn for themselves.
   - As early as possible, give your child the gift of READING. Higher education does not always take place in expensive colleges and universities. Learning to read widely and deeply is a key to success for anyone. If you can't provide the above things for your child, find those in the community who can.

Hello Mr. Ramos, I wanted to share the experience I left in my survey with you. I had such a great, life-changing experience with POM. I am forever grateful to you for this program. Wednesday night POM classes with Mr. Rothford and Mrs. Collins was the greatest thing that could've happened to my family and me. My family was so broken that I honestly feel that if classes had not started when they did, I would be in jail, my daughter would have attempted or committed suicide, or my kids would have been taken by CWS [Child Welfare Services], or all the above. Even though POM was explained at orientation, I went into it thinking it was going to help me deal with my 'bad kids'. It was a reality check knowing that the chaos and hurt was because basically I allowed it. I've learned that I am the start of the change in my family. I've learned to think before I speak or act and sometimes it's best to address situations the next day. I've learned that apologizing when I'm wrong goes a long way. I started applying things I learned in POM right away and things were still all over the place at home. Halfway through I thought, 'OMG what's the point?' But at the eighth class I thought about not only how I am now compared to before POM, but my daughters as well, and we are making changes for the better. We still have a lot of growing to do. But everyone seems to be in a much better place. There's not as much chaos and anger. We can now go days or even a week without a blow up at home. Before they used to happen at least once a day, sometimes two. And when they do happen, it's NOTHING compared to what it used to be. There was yelling, throwing things, broken mirrors, physical contact, slamming doors, punching holes in the wall…now, at its worst, it's maybe thirty seconds of yelling back and forth…There's still a long road ahead of us, but with the help of POM, now we're on the right road. At the third class we were given an assignment of writing a letter to those we feel we needed to apologize to. I wrote my letters to my daughters…it was very hard to apologize and hold myself accountable for not being the person I should've been and doing or allowing the bad things that have been going on. When I got home, I gave the letters to my daughters…my…daughter who has always acted out more and that I mentioned I felt she would commit suicide…came into my room and said, 'Mom, thank you. I love you.' I kissed her and said 'you're welcome and I'm sorry for everything.' As I hugged her and she cried, I reassured her that everything was going to be okay…and I would never leave her side. This morning as we were getting ready her whole attitude was different. She was calmer, she didn't seem so defensive…just before we left home this morning she said, 'My new goal in life is to get to heaven' and she was serious! The negative things that are now almost non-existent, and the positive things that have happened so far, wouldn't have if I wouldn't have started POM. Mr. Ramos… Mr. Rothford and Mrs. Collins, I truly thank you from the bottom of my heart. You may not realize it, but you saved my family! – Adrianna Guzman

6.

Reconciliation

To say that ALL families have problems may be a stretch. I don't know. To be safe, let me say that most, if not all, families encounter problems of one kind or another at one time or another. Thus, family problems, as it were, are nothing unusual. Nothing to fear, be surprised by, or unexpected. Different families experience different kinds of problems in various degrees and circumstances.

These days we are much more aware of family problems. And for better or worse, we are much more exposed to what in times past would be known as "family secrets". But the issue is not the fact that families have problems. The issue is what we do about them. It's about how we handle them. How do we go about reconciling differences, family falling-out's, arguments, heated confrontations, and offensive words or actions?

To answer these questions, there is a story I like to use that I believe provides a great example for guidance in the principles of wisdom for handling difficult situations.

The story is one many people are familiar with, called "The Prodigal Son". (1)

However, I believe who ever titled this story *The Prodigal Son* got it wrong. They missed the point of the story, which is not about the son, but rather it is about what I call The Great Father.

The story starts by saying, *"There was a certain man who had two sons..."* That "certain man" is what the story is about. If you're not familiar with this story, allow me to share a paraphrased version of it here:

One day, the younger of the father's two sons comes to his father and declares that he wants all his inheritance now. Apparently, he's not happy living at home and/or working for his father and wants to go out on his own to do his own thing. The father does not argue, grants his son his inheritance, and the son leaves to take a *journey to a far country*. At some point thereafter the son squanders all his inheritance. He blows it on drink, drugs, prostitutes, and all manner of the "party life". Eventually he finds himself homeless, broke, and starving in a pigpen eating with the pigs. In that tired and broken place, the story says, *he came to himself* and said (my paraphrase), *what the heck am I doing here working and eating with pigs? My father has servants who have plenty to eat...I could go home...*

Now, let me pause here and ask you a question. I want you to stop for a moment and consider how many runaways, rebellious youth, are out in the streets right now...and possibly have *come to themselves*, because they are tired of being out there on their own, and in that broken condition can truly say, *"I could go home"?* It saddens me to say, not many.

You see, the reason the prodigal son could say, "I could go home," is because he knew what kind of father he had. He knew the type of man his father was. He knew his character. And that is what the story is about. The Great Father. The kind Father. The loving Father. The wise Father patiently hoping for the return of his lost son.

And so, the son gets up and begins his journey back home. When he is getting closer to home, his father sees his son *afar off* and runs to his son before he reaches home and showers him with hugs and kisses. He does not rigidly stand there with an "I told you so" attitude. Or the snide remark, "I knew you'd be back." He doesn't start *shoulding* on him, ("You should've never left," "You shouldn't have done that," "You should have listened to me," etc.) Nor does the father shame him like so many parents do when the wayward son or daughter returns.

The son, being ashamed of himself, kneels before his father and begins to tell his father he has really screwed up and is no longer worthy to be his son. He does not ask to be taken back as a son, but rather in the lowest rank of a slave. However, the father would have none of that and turns to his servants and tells them to bring the best robe, the family ring to place on his son's finger and new shoes to wear, and then says, *"and bring the fatted calf, kill it and cook it so we can eat and celebrate the return of my lost son!"*

Let me pause again here and point out a few things that are very significant about the time, place, and culture in which this story is being told.

- Under Jewish law a father of this stature was not allowed to leave, let alone run, from his property any time he liked.
- The fact that he saw and ran to his son when he was "afar off" shows that he apparently had been waiting and watching for his son to return.
- Before the son can finish asking to come home as a servant, the father cuts him off and tells the servants to bring a robe, which at that time and culture stands for honor; the ring signifies authority; the shoes signify the status only a son would receive as slaves did not get to wear shoes because they were a sign of freedom.(2)

But the story does not end there...

Now the elder son, who had been working out in the fields, is on his way home and hears music, dancing, laughter, and the sounds of joy. He comes upon one of the servants and asks, *"What's happening?"* The servant replies, *"Oh, your father is throwing a party!"* *"Oh, yeah. Why?"* Again, the servant replies, *"The party is to celebrate your brother who has returned home!"*

At this the elder son becomes furious! *"What? Why that lousy, no-good, rebellious idiot"* (my speculative words), and on and on he goes criticizing his brother. As the elder son is express-ing his anger and refusing to join the party, the father, who is inside enjoying the party, sees his son outside having his tantrum. So, what does the father do? Or, better yet, what doesn't he do? He doesn't say, *"Oh get over yourself."* Or, *"Stop whining and thinking about yourself."* Or, *"Stop acting like a spoiled brat!"* No. This is a great Father.

He goes out to his son and calmly asks him, *"What's wrong?"* The son in anger says, *"All these years I have been with you faithfully working hard and I have never disobeyed you or done the things like your son who wasted all you gave him. And yet you throw him a party and kill the fatted calf? You never did that for me. You never gave me a calf to celebrate with my friends."*

After patiently listening to his elder son's rant, the father ex-plains to him, *"Son, everything I own, everything I have is yours and has always been yours. But your brother was lost, spiritually dead, and gone. But now he has awakened and returned to himself and to us and that is something we must rejoice in and celebrate."*

This is what the story is about. A Great Father that has:

- Unconditional love for his rebellious son.
- Patience in the heartache of waiting for his son to hopefully reach the hardship of life that would cause him to repent and come back home.

- Emotional maturity of pre-forgiveness. He obviously had already forgiven his son as demonstrated by initiating the reconciliation by running to him and hugging, kissing, receiving, and honoring him as his son and not a servant.
- Generosity in throwing a party by using the "fatted calf", which in those days signified wealth.
- Principles of humility, patience, kindness, and forgiveness that demonstrated to the self-righteous, jealous son how to reconcile a broken family relationship.

You may not have experienced the exact circumstances of the above story, but I submit that the same principles apply when we find ourselves in a strained, estranged, or broken parent-child relationship that occur for one reason or another.

The easy (and I will add dysfunctional) thing to do is to sweep it under the proverbial rug. Ignore the issue or the other person. Not talk about what happened. Take a posture of denial, pride, fear, anxiety, or anger, all of which are barriers to producing a healthy reconciliation.

We probably all know friends, or family members who have suppressed some very deep emotional issues for years. Perhaps you have suppressed some difficult issues yourself. But what we know about suppressed emotions is that they cause depression, and/or eventually come out in ugly ways oftentimes towards innocent people we love and people who love us, and round and round the dysfunctional cycle goes and the hurts, violations, and deep wounds are never resolved, and trust is never restored.

These are the kinds of issues I deal with and speak to in POM with parents to encourage them to stop avoiding and start addressing their family relationship issues, beginning with themselves.

This is what leadership is all about. Looking within to see where I might be part of the problem I'm having in any context at work, family of origin, extended family, or at home. Depending on the circumstances this can be a very challenging and difficult process. Yet, the rewards of practicing the principles of reconciliation are priceless.

After parents have what I call "the POM experience" they are willing and ready to initiate the reconciliation process. Here are a few examples:

I want to thank you for a very awesome class…I never was a mother to my children. I didn't have the tools or patience to even be one. You have helped me by giving me the tools and motivation to begin this new life. I'm so excited to get out and become a mother to my children. Thank you, Mr. Ramos, for helping me and my children's life.
– Tiffany Lujan

They say, like father, like son. My dad was a man of few words like me. My son sits in a jail cell. I feel I have failed him. I now realize I haven't. I plan to visit him and apologize to him. To tell him I love him, care about him, and will not give up on him.
– Jim Compton

I have identified and accepted my mistakes in raising my children. There is no excuse. I can no longer think that being a single parent is a handicap. Now when I return home, I'm going to tell the kids I'm sorry, you were right, I was wrong, please forgive me for the yelling and not paying attention and spending quality time doing things together.
– Audrey Brass

Dear Richard, my wife and I took the Parents on a Mission program two years ago with your brother Tony and it changed the relationship with our two sons for good. – Hector Ruvalcaba

Over the years I have received numerous letters and testimonials of family, parent-child reconciliation, and transformation as expressed in these examples. It gives me such great joy, but more importantly, it is the fuel that continues to ignite my passion for continuing to reach out, recruit, and develop more Parents on a Mission.

I felt insecure and intimidated. I said to myself, "I don't have children and I don't want children. How exactly am I going to spin this?" I kept telling myself this as I sat in Day One of Parents on a Mission Instructor's Course. Over the next three days, I mostly listened. I heard the stories and perspectives of all the would-be instructors. The more comfortable we got with each other, the atmosphere felt... lighter and warm. It became a safe space for other adults to share stories and learn from each other. By Day Three, nearly everyone had shared something about themselves that was very close to their hearts.

My classmates shared their love for their children. How their relationships have improved as they confronted their own traumas. Almost everyone has a story about wanting to be better parents than the generations before them. Learning to heal from deep emotional pain is how we ensure we don't hurt the people around us.

At the very end of Day Three, I decided to speak up as the day was coming to an end. The long and short of it is this: My father was a real shit stain. He "parented" the best he could with what he had but still chose to remain ignorant. The more I reflect, the worse it gets. He was dead to me long before he actually died. I simply couldn't give him anything more, so I broke away. I only hope that in the end, someone was kind to him. I wish there was someone, somewhere, at some point in his life that could have intervened. Maybe someone that he listened to could have urged him to help himself. Maybe I could have had a chance at knowing who my father was. I only got to know the drunk. I shared in class painful memories and how I have learned to overcome obstacles. Maybe sharing my story and my perspective will lead a dad back to their kid and give them a shot at something I never had with mine.

I was not the last person to share that day. Frank spoke up too. Frank and I are the same age, and our birthdays are only weeks apart. He has two young kids, a girl and a boy. He is a military vet and served tours overseas. Despite having a rough upbringing, he never blames anyone but himself. And he always smiles. Frank did not say much either, like me. When Frank was six years old, his mom locked him and his two younger sisters in a room. Mom left the house, and the kids were alone. One sister was three years old and the youngest was a toddler. Frank was playing with a lighter and accidentally set the blankets on the bed on fire, which set fire to the rest of the room. His three-year-old sister didn't make it. The mom blamed six-year-old Frank and abandoned him and his surviving sister in a warehouse. They were alone for days. Frank sobbed. It was the first time in his life he had shared that story. For the last 32 years, he alone, carried the overwhelming shame and guilt of the death of his little sister. He told himself every day it was his fault and that he killed her.

To serve others, whether that be children, family, or your community, we must be healthy and happy with ourselves. Trauma is not what happens to us, it's what happens inside of us. The only way to move past the pain is to acknowledge it and walk through it. Your role as an instructor is to maintain an environment that promotes those moments of vulnerability and human connection. – Sondra Ballegeer, Parole Release Case Manager – Division of Parole, Four Mile Correctional Center, Canon City, Colorado

7.

How to Win Loyalty

Madness is a strong word, but the more I learn about what our children are being taught, and when, the more I stand by that choice. Parents, have you heard what our kids are being told? Have you seen what's being put in front of them? I thought it was illegal to make indecent material available to minors…I suggest you explore the material sex educators have created for kids…Do you want instructors, whose personal values might be at odds with yours, to encourage your kids to question what they've been taught at home and in church…Wake up America: This is one giant hoax…Make no mistake: this is a battle, and the battleground is our kids' minds and values." – Miriam Grossman, M.D., You're Teaching My Child What? – A Physician Expose the Lies of Sex Education and How They Harm your Child.

If you take nothing else away from reading this book, PLEASE hear me on this…it is the crux…the bottom line…the heart and soul of my POM message:

What every parent in America (and perhaps the world) must understand is that you are in a daily competition for the hearts, minds, and loyalty of your children. If you don't understand that—or are unaware of that—you're not even in the game. Therefore, Mom and Dad, you need to wake up and get in the game because what's at stake is your children's loyalty and the main question—the challenge—you should be concerned with is: Who is going to win the battle for loyalty? And if you are taking your children's loyalty for granted, you are making a huge mistake.

Competition from Public School Policy

The explicit undermining of parents' authority that is going on in many public schools today is almost too much to believe. The fact that there are actual elected school board members, (1) teachers, and in some case judges, (2) impeding the right of parents to be involved in the education of their children and what their children are being taught, is astounding to me. One of the newer, and worst policies, is this idea being fed to children that they should keep secrets from their parents about life-changing issues they are dealing with. The excuse and rationale from the school is that this is being done for the sake of the child, to protect them from the harm that will come if their parents are told about their personal struggles with something as important as gender identity. (3) What an insult. The audacity for the school to think they know better than a child's parent about what to do and how to handle such a major and life-changing issue. But this (amongst other things parents are outraged about) is what is taking place in our day and age of what public education has become.

College campuses became a battleground of ideologies and American culture wars back in the early 1960s (4) marked by student protests, urban riots, and violence. For the most part since that time the culture wars were kept at the college and political levels of debate. However, after a long and continued slow and steady battle over the past forty years, we now are witnessing the spread of this ongoing culture clash at every level of society, reaching our children on the high school, middle school, and elementary school campus:

> "Over time, the scholarship that began in the universities trickled down to the primary and secondary education systems. The result is that thousands of public schools are now training American schoolchildren, explicitly or implicitly, to see the world through the lens of critical pedagogy." (5)

Critical pedagogy is a term that refers to a political point of view regarding how students should be educated. Let me be clear, I don't mean to go down a rabbit hole of politics here. That is not the purpose of POM. But, to keep in line with this chapter's subject of loyalty, my purpose is to awaken parents to what is taking place with their children in the public schools. To be fair, if you are aware of and in agreement with the philosophical and political positions that school boards and legislatures (like here in California) have assumed, then end of discussion. That is your prerogative as parents. However, like many of the parents that I have met and spoken to, many parents, if not most of them, are not aware of what is taking place in school with the hearts, minds, and loyalties of their children from a moral values and worldview perspective.

We witnessed this during the COVID-19 pandemic when schools were shut down and children were attending school via ZOOM. This led to parents at home who began to over-hear what teachers were saying and teaching, which resulted in the parent protests at school board meetings referred to above. Parents expressed outrage and disapproval with sub-ject matter they felt was inappropriate for elementary school children. The issues of sex education and gender identity are front and center as we are all hearing and seeing. To say these are important issues is an understatement. These subjects and realities are loaded with all kinds of opinions and moral ques-tions that parents do not want their children discussing in the schoolhouse. Parents have not given their consent for teach-ers, counselors, or other social specialists to teach or discuss these adult topics and inculcate the minds of their children with a point of view that they may not agree with. To think that children need parental consent to receive an aspirin from a school nurse or to go on a field trip with their teacher and classmates, but need no parental consent to discuss sex, abor-tion, and gender identity is the height of hypocrisy and an ethical violation of parental authority and rights. And it does not stop with sex and gender identity but also includes politi-cizing the hearts and minds of public school children. Author Christopher Rufo writes:

"The method of critical pedagogy is now mandatory statewide. After releasing the model curriculum, the California state legislature quickly passed a bill making ethnic studies a graduation requirement for all high school students....implicit in every step in the process...is a transfer of power from parents, families, and citizens to the bureaucratic class: administrators, counselors, consultants, specialists, advisors, and paper-pushers." (6)

Parents are not only being undermined but we are also being betrayed. We cannot count on our institutions to support or honor the values that we choose to live by and teach to our own children. It truly is an intentional "transfer of power" away from us. This anti-parent influence is essentially all around us. And with the advancement of technology, the hard fact is that there is no escaping it. That's the bad news. But the good news is there is a way parents can counter its influence, which I will address shortly.

The power of technology and the 4Ms in the heads-down generation

In addition, we are living in a technology age that we have never experienced before, and it is only going to get more and more intrusive in every aspect of our family, work, education, and community relationships. We are not only being influenced but becoming addicted to it. Take for example our smart phones. It seems so many just can't put it down. Can't stop looking at it. Can't get enough of messaging, checking, and scrolling and clicking. It's a "heads-down" generation. Heads down in the car, heads down in the classroom, at the dinner table, in the living room, at the beach, at the airport, on the plane, on the bus, while standing in line, in the restaurant, and in the bedroom for heaven's sake! The same happens with even the youngest of children, addicted to their tablets and/ or their parents' smart phones to be entertained. Here is one teacher's observation of the effect this is having on children, in an email I received:

> "Yesterday, I shut down class about five minutes early and told my students I wanted them to just sit and talk to one another. Several of them immediately opened their laptops and began navigating to their favorite computer game.
>
> I said, "No, no laptops. I want you to have face-to-face conversations right now."
>
> After a collective groan went up, I observed something both wonderful and alarming. For the next few minutes, a couple of tables came alive with conversation. They looked at each other in the eyes and talked with great enthusiasm and interest. It was beautiful to watch and listen to.
>
> However, many students were deflated. They did not know what to do without some sort of entertainment from a device. A couple of them put their heads down

and avoided eye contact with anyone. I went around the room to those students and tried to engage with them. Some of them mustered a few words, but most didn't know what to do.

I share this story as a wake-up call for parents, grand-parents, and guardians. It's tragic to me that a large percentage of today's youth do not know how to have real conversation, but it's not their fault. It is our re-sponsibility as adults to lead by example and hold our kids accountable. Unplug every day, talk, and listen to your children. Getting lost in a device does not help them cope with and overcome the things they're go-ing through mentally, emotionally, and spiritually. All it causes is isolation and depression. They need rela-tionships; they need you."

The 4Ms

In general, your competition comes from four sources that I call the 4Ms:

- Music
- Movies
- Magazines
- Media

None of us can escape this constant, 24/7/365 bombardment of noise, news, and nuisance. That's not to say that I don't enjoy music, watch movies, listen to the news, or use social media. That's not my point. The issue is the messaging and the mesmerizing that is interfering with our relationships and ability to have a simple conversation with our children.

Have you ever thought about the messages in the music your kids listen to constantly? Many parents have no idea of the lyrics to the songs their kids listen to. What types of movies are your kids watching? And what is the message your children are being influenced by? The same goes for the messaging from regular TV programs that many parents are put off by, but that are socially normalizing our children. And with today's access to the internet via computers and social media via smart phones, the negative influencers have become all too obvious. This is part of what Dr. Neufeld and Dr. Maté are referring to when they say in their book I referred to earlier, *"parenthood is being undermined. We face much insidious competition that would draw our children away from us while, simultaneously, we are drawn away from parenthood."*

In their book, *The Violence Project: How to Stop a Mass Shooting Epidemic*, authors Jillian Peterson and James Densley found that because of the influence of social media on teens, their number one goal for success is to become famous by the number of likes they receive from their followers and how many followers imitate them on social media platforms like TikTok:

> "One 2011 study found that a desire for fame solely for the sake of being famous was the most popular future goal among American preadolescents, overshadowing

hopes for financial success, achievement, or a sense of community…one-fourth of Millennials would quit their jobs to become famous. One in twelve would detach themselves from their families for fame.…according to our data, the past decade has seen a rise in shootings motivated by fame-seeking, and the idolization of fame drives nearly one in ten of all mass shooters. (7)

Again, this is not to say that all uses of social media are bad. And I am not advocating that parents remove or disallow all uses of music, movies, and social media from their children. As a matter of fact, that would probably be counterproductive. The parental message I am advocating here is not about abstention from, but about awareness of, the daily competition we face. Parents need to get in the game!

Lessons on loyalty from a teenage gang member

Youth street gangs are among the many negative lifestyle choices parents worry about with raising children in a gang-culture neighborhood or school environment. Having grown up in this kind of environment myself, I know of the temptation and pressure to fit in, be cool, belong, and "be down," as the saying goes.

Being in a gang is all about loyalty. That's the mentality: loyalty to your homeboys/girls and loyalty to your hood. That's what you are committing yourself to when you decide to join a street gang. But the question this begs is, why? Why does a young girl or a young boy make this kind of choice? As it turns out, the answer is quite simple as expressed by this fourteen-year-old girl gang member, in her own words and exactly as she wrote it:

"EVERYONE WANTS TO KNOW WHY. WHY DID YOU JOIN? YOU HAVE A FAMILY WHO LOVES AND CARES FOR YOU, WHY MIJA WHY? I JOINED BECAUSE WHEN I WAS A LIL GURL ALOT SHYT HAPPENED TO ME THAT NOBODY KNOWS ABOUT AND I HAVE KEPT INSIDE OF ME ALL THYZ TYME. NOWBODY LISTENED TO ME AND WHEN THEY DID, THEY SAID I WAS LYING. DRUG ADDICT DAD AND WORK ALCOHOLIC MOM, NO BROTHERS, NO SISTERS, A STEP DAD THAT ONLY WANTS TO TOUCH ME. AND A BABYSITER WHOSE SON DID TOUCH ME. MY MOM ALWAYS RIPPING ME OUT OF FAMILIES THAT I THOUGHT WERE MINE, IT WAS ALL LIES.

LIVING IN THA GHETTO WONDERING WHY? CAN YOU TELL ME WHY? CAN YOU TELL ME WHY I WAS BORN IN THIS LIFE OF SEX DRUGS AND ALCOHOL, BACK STABBING OF MY SO CALLED REAL FAMILY? I WAS JUST A LIL GURL DANM. THOSE MEMORIES ARE WITH ME FOREVER I'M SCARED TO LIVE LIFE I'M SCARED TO TRUST N-E BODY, I'M SCARED.

SO WHY DID I JOIN? I JOINED BECAUSE I NEEDED SUMONE AND THEY WERE THE ONLY ONES THERE. I NEEDED SUMONE TO MAKE ME FEEL WANTED AND I NEEDED SUMONE TO CARE. THAT'S WHY."

Here in her testimony this young girl answers the three questions that have eluded scholars, community authorities, and law enforcement at the federal, state, and local levels: 1) What is a gang? 2) Why do kids join gangs? 3) What is the best method of preventing kids from joining gangs? This young lady simply tells us that: 1) a gang is a replacement for the family; 2) the reason kids join gangs is because they can't trust their own family to be loyal to them; and 3) the best method for preventing kids from joining gangs is to help parents be better parents. It's just that simple and does not require millions of dollars for more studies, more laws, more school rules, or more police on the street to figure this out.

In addition to the above three answers, she also offers some important lessons and insights regarding family relationships and loyalty:

- Family instability breeds insecurity and confusion.
- Violated personal trust causes suppressed secrets that breed disloyalty.
- Children who don't feel they belong feel scared and alone.
- Children who have no sense of being respected feel silenced.
- Children given no value feel cheap.

- Children given no family purpose will look for one somewhere else.
- Dysfunctional families cause misplaced trust.
- A decision of misplaced loyalty is an issue of trust lost by the family.
- Kids give away their loyalty as a second choice, not as their first choice.
- Initially, every child desires to give their loyalty to their parents, but parents must be willing to pay the price to win/earn it.
- When parents win the loyalty of their children it gives them the strength to say "no" to peer pressure because their peers are asking for a loyalty already given away to their first family.
- Parents are competing every day in many ways for the loyalty of their children and the best way to win this competition is to build relationships of trust.

From my perspective, communities have been asking the wrong question, and this has led to taking the wrong approach in addressing youth and local street gangs. The question should not be, *Why do kids join gangs*…but rather, *Why do most kids not join gangs?* And the answer is: Most kids don't join gangs due to the type of family culture they are raised in and their strong and healthy relationship with their parents.

"Studies have been unequivocal in their findings that the best protection for a child, even through adolescence, is a strong attachment with an adult [mentor]. The most impressive of these studies involved ninety thousand adolescents from eighty different communities chosen to make the sample as representative of the United States as possible. The primary finding was that teenagers with strong emotional ties to their parents were much less likely to exhibit drug and alcohol problems, attempt suicide, or engage in violent behavior and early sexual activity. Such adolescents, in other words, were at greatly reduced risk for the problems that stem from being defended against vulnerability. Shielding them from stress and protecting their emotional health and functioning were strong attachments with their parents." (8)

Therefore, the best *prevention* strategy communities can invest in is emphasizing, supporting, and strengthening parental authority and leadership in the home, rather than what many schools, media, and government seem to be doing these days to undermine parental authority and influence with their children, as I have outlined here and above. (9)

So, how can parents defeat their competition from the undermining of schools, government, the influence of social media, the 4Ms, and gangs, and win the loyalty of their children? In POM we share five very simple methods.

Family History, Tradition, and Legacy

The key factor in developing loyalty is to meet the basic human need to belong. As social beings we all have this innate desire to be a part of something meaningful. A desire to find our place in the world. A desire to pledge our loyalty to something bigger than ourselves. A desire to belong. Our family of origin is the first place we seek to fulfill this need for rootedness, attachment, and connectedness to help us gain an understanding of the world. (10) A 2010 study showed that just the exercise of thinking about our ancestors could have a positive effect on our intellectual performance, process of social identity, family cohesion, and self-regulation. (11)

Below is an exercise I use to help parents think about their family history, traditions, and legacy. I explain that this is an exercise that requires time for reflection and should not be completed in class. I am simply introducing the idea as one way to inspire them to give deep thought to describing their family, to ask: Who are we? What is our family about? What matters to us? And more importantly, what do we want our family legacy to be for our children and grandchildren? If parents have children from ten years old and up (or whatever age they feel appropriate), I encourage them to include their children in developing their family legacy. (12) This serves as a powerful way to engage children in anchoring their heart to a cause, a purpose, and to be proud of their family heritage and history.

As you see in the illustration below, I ask the parents to use their last name as an acronym along the left-hand side of the paper. Each letter in their last name is used to describe who their family is and what their legacy is about. If they have multiple last names or have been divorced, etc. I instruct them to decide which last name they feel will best be useful for describing their family legacy.

> Revolutionary
>
> Advocate
>
> Mission
>
> Original
>
> Spiritual

This may seem like a simple tool, but I have seen many families take this exercise to heart with their children and come away with a very positive experience that moves them closer to attachment, winning, and earning the loyalty of their children.

A second tool I suggest to parents for winning loyalty is the creation of a family mission statement. I learned the value of this many years ago from one of my book-mentors, Stephen R. Covey. (13) Developing a family mission statement with your children I believe is one of the best leadership activities parents can use to give their children a sense of belonging, value, purpose, and guidance for their life. This probably seems like the same thing as the legacy exercise I just shared. However, there is a distinct difference: The legacy exercise is about a long-term vision. Its focus is the future and something we want to pass on from generation to generation. The mission statement is more about right now. It provides guidance on a daily basis towards specific values, roles, and goals and the priorities and principles to practice for achieving our goals.

How to Develop a Family Mission Statement

There are four basic steps in this process. (14) You may prefer a different process for your family. That's fine. You know what will work best with your family. You might be in a situation where your kids are still very young—maybe too young to participate in this first iteration of your mission as a family. Or perhaps you're hearing this for the first time and your children are adults and no longer living at home. Or maybe you have a blended family (as I do, so we developed the Ramos/Gonzalez family mission statement many years ago). There are any number of different family situations you could be in, but the important thing is that you see the value of taking a more formal approach of coming together as a family to discuss and develop a mission that speaks to all your (immediate) family members. Remember your purpose: to win the hearts, mind, and loyalty of your children.

Step 1. Plan to gather your family on a day, time, and place with no distractions. Give your children a heads-up at least a few days beforehand so they won't make any plans for that day and time. It's not a good idea to tell them a day ahead of time or the morning of the meeting. For example: Let's say the best time for your family would be on a Saturday morning. (15) You then let them know on Tuesday or Wednesday that you want to have an hour of their time to talk about an idea you learned about developing a family mission statement and you would like to begin the process on Saturday. The goal here is to get a commitment of date and time.

Step 2. On that Saturday morning you briefly explain what a family mission statement is, its purpose, and why you think it's a good thing for your family. Before proceeding to start developing the mission statement you ask if they have any questions or comments. You listen until everyone has had a chance to speak. (Depending on your children, they may have nothing to say at this point, or a lot to say. No worries or hurries.)

Now you're ready to lead the discussion. If your wife/husband or significant other, or one of your children, is able, have one of them take notes. Begin by asking for input to questions like the following. These are only suggestions. You don't have to ask them all necessarily:

- What is the purpose of our family?
- What are we best at as a family?
- What kind of family do we want to be?
- What kind of home do we want people to find when they visit us?
- What are the things we feel are most important to our family?
- What are our highest priorities and goals?

- What are our unique talents and gifts we can contribute to others?
- What values do we want to live by (honesty, fairness, trust, etc.)
- What are our responsibilities to our neighborhood and community?

Step 3. Based on the input from all family members to the questions above, designate someone (usually a parent) to begin to write a first draft of your mission statement.

- Try to combine everyone's thoughts.
- Ask for help with the wording if needed.
- Use your imagination and don't worry about length or format at this point.
- Basic characteristics of the mission statement:
- Includes characteristics of family culture (loving, kind, giving, etc.)
- Speaks to the effect of the mission statement upon the family (stronger, more spiritual, patient, etc.)
- States a meaningful purpose (to serve the community, etc.)
- Identifies a family's source of strength (faith, integrity, principles, etc.)

Step 4. Call another family meeting (Don't wait too long or you'll lose any excitement or momentum you created in the first meeting). Share the first draft to get feedback and any suggestions for edits or corrections. Work on the final draft together until everyone is satisfied with the wording of the final version.

Step 5. (Optional) This is a chance for yours or your children's creativity. How do you want to display the family mission statement? Do you want to make it into a nicely lettered graphic design and frame it to display on a wall in your home? Do you want to print it on a business card with a family logo to give to each of your children to carry with them? Do you want to create a digital version you can all put on your phones?

There are a lot of options, but the main thing is to find a way to put the mission statement in front of your children. Give it significance. Read it together and most of all live it together.

Sample Family Mission Statements:

"The mission of our family is to create a nurturing place of order, truth, love, happiness and relaxation, and to provide opportunities for each person to become responsibly independent and effectively interdependent in order to achieve worthwhile purposes."

"Our family mission is to love each other… To help each other… To believe in each other…To wisely use our time, talents, and resources to bless others… To worship together…Forever."

Our family mission is to:

- Establish a positive influence in the community through our example of love for God and one another.

- Build fun, honest, and trusting relationships through quality time and communication with each other.
- Support one another with respect, participation, understanding, and forgiveness.
- Develop an open, relaxing, clean, and beautiful home that everyone is drawn to.
- Inspire one another to set goals that help us reach our God-given potential individually and as a family. (16)

The Power of High Touch in a High-Tech World

Another tool we teach in POM is what I call the power of *High Touch*

When was the last time you sat down, and hand-wrote a letter? A time invested in careful thought about how you wanted to express your feelings, your heartfelt emotions, possibly rewriting it until you have expressed yourself with just the right words? The reason that we invest this focused time to write is because intuitively we know that words have power.

In today's high-tech world we have become accustomed to communicating via the convenience of texting and email. Nothing wrong with that. However, there is still something special…something deeper and a little more powerful about handwritten words. If you have ever written a poem, a song, or a love letter, you know what I mean. It takes focused concentration for an extended period of time. As Mark Twain is reported to have said, *"I apologize for the long letter. I didn't have time to write a short one."* That's because to write a short meaningful letter requires a lot of time for thoughtfulness.

This tool is another effective way to win loyalty. It may seem simplistic but that short (or long) handwritten note your child finds in their lunch bag, sports bag, or receives in the mail can go a long way in building trust and winning the heart, mind, and loyalty of your child.

My five children were all very athletically inclined when they were growing up. That allowed me the opportunity to write a short letter or note to them and stick in their helmet, baseball or basketball shoes, ballet shoes, or cheerleading bag. In that letter I would encourage them on their performance and assure them that their mom and I would be watching and cheering them on. I know they appreciated that gesture and it did (and still does) help build our relationship. These days we still practice the handwritten words with each other in cards on birthdays, holidays, and special occasions expressing ourselves in writing in addition to the words that are already in the store-bought card. I know how much their words mean to me and I'm sure they feel the same way about my handwritten words to them.

These kinds of things, expressing our love and appreciation, never get old. They never become unnecessary or undervalued. We are social beings with physical, emotional, psychological, and spiritual needs. Parents should not undervalue their role in meeting these needs for their children regardless of their age, distance, or because of a strained relationship due to an argument or something else that may hold you back from reaching out in this manner if needed.

The secret prevention weapon hidden in every home

A fourth suggestion we make regarding winning loyalty is encouraging parent heroes in the home. I call it "the secret prevention weapon hidden in every home" because I believe children who look up to their parents as heroes *almost always* choose loyalty to family over choosing loyalty to negative influences and lifestyles. (17)

Definition of a "hero"

- A "hero" is someone bigger than life.
- Someone to look up to.
- Someone who is what I want to be.
- Someone who does great things to help others.
- Someone who I can trust and depend upon to always be there when I need them.
- Someone who is loved by all.

With this definition, we have just described "Superman/woman", but that is what a hero is in a sense. An almost mythical, mystery kind of a person, beyond the ordinary, unlike the rest of us, or so we think anyway, and somehow it almost doesn't matter whether it is true or not or whether they really exist or not, because we can still draw inspiration from this figure we have in our heart and mind as a personal source of inspiration.

> "We cannot live fully without heroes, for they are the stars to guide us upward. They are the peaks on our human mountains. Not only do they personify what we can be, but they also urge us to be. Heroes are who we can become, if we diligently pursue our ideas ...Heroes are those who have changed history for the better....Their deeds are not done for the honor, but for the duty..." – Frank Smith

Of course, our children will also draw inspiration from other heroes they may have such as rock stars, movie stars, and sports stars. That is common and nothing to necessarily worry about. But my point here is to inspire moms and dads to see themselves as heroes as well and have a desire to ultimately be the main hero in the life of their children as they grow older.

At this point I hope you are saying to yourself: "Okay, Richard. I want to be the hero of my children...how do I do that?" I'm glad you asked.

I suppose there are a lot of ways to be a parent hero. However, I'm not trying to make this difficult with an exhaustive list of credentials or qualifying attributes for being a hero. What I share in POM are three very basic principles that any parent can do.

1. **Priorities.** As adults we choose our priorities. Part of being a hero to our children is the consistent choice of investing time in our children's activities as first, important, and top priority.

   I believe our children understand that because of work and other responsibilities we may have that we can't always get to every event they are involved in. Nevertheless, we consistently and gladly participate as much as possible to be supportive and show our interest and pride for them as they are performing or being recognized in one way or another. It means so much to them, especially when we go out of our way and make a special effort to be present

   Sometimes single parents (or both parents) that have more than one job say they "don't have time" to show up. But, as I said, kids understand legitimate reasons why a parent might not be able to attend a game, a performance, etc. What they get sad about is when they know you are choosing not to be there. When you choose not to make time. It's not that we don't have time. Everybody has time. It's choosing to make time for our children that matters, and they know the difference when we choose not to, and when we choose to make time for them. What we choose to give our time to says a lot about our life priorities and the hero parent chooses investment of time in their children as a priority.

2. **Integrity.** We don't have to be perfect, just honest, to win the love and respect of our children and humble enough to apologize when we make mistakes.

   I have had the blessing of having my children tell me or write about me as their hero. It is a very rewarding thing to hear and feel from your child. Yet, the thing is that I know the real me. My kids know the real me. And the real me is far from perfect. Nevertheless, they still consider me their hero. How can that be? It's simple really. What makes us heroes is not that we are perfect parents, but rather that we are honest parents. That we have integrity. That we own up to our mistakes and failures. We look our children in the eye when we have done the wrong thing, said the wrong thing, acted in a wrong way, and we sincerely apologize. That is how an imperfect parent can still be the hero of their children and win their loyalty.

3. **Crisis.** It may not seem like a crisis to us, but if it is important to them, in those hard times we are there for them. We may not have all the answers or know the right words to speak, but we can show up in the crisis of life and often that is all that is needed.

   Throughout the lives of each of my children I have watched them and experienced with them disappointment, failure, let-down, heartbreak, and grief. It is one of the painful things about loving your children so much—when they hurt...you hurt. Maybe even more at times because you never want to see your children sad, crying, and brokenhearted for one reason or another. In that moment you want to take their pain away. You want to take their place. You want to say and do the right thing to make it all better. But the reality is, you can't. But even if you can't take the pain away in the moment, you can be there; quietly, calmly, empathetically. They appreciate that. They always remember that, and it goes a long way in earning trust, respect, and loyalty.

In the case of my sons, it was usually after a disappointing loss in sports. For my daughters it was usually a hard breakup, let-down, or betrayal by a boyfriend. And the worst crisis, for me and all of them, was the loss of their mother to breast cancer in 1994 when they were all relatively young. Obviously, this was a very traumatic and very hard time for our family and the type of crisis that never really heals or goes away… you just learn to live with it in a better and healthier way. You make sure you don't let it overwhelm you to the point of completely taking away the quality of life that the loved one you lost would want you to maintain even though they are no longer here.

This lifetime psychological and spiritual process that requires mature leadership is at the heart of what Parents on a Mission is all about. In these sensitive and tough times, it's not our words, so much as our presence, that makes the difference in being seen as a hero to our children.

Conclusion

As of this writing (August 2023), I just finished watching the first debate of presidential candidates vying for the Republican nomination to run in the 2024 election against the incumbent, President Biden (or another candidate should Biden not be nominated again by the Democratic party).

The reason I mention this is because of the questions that are always asked by the moderators in these presidential debates, specifically: *What are you, as President, going to do about...* and then the debate moderators go on to name some pressing issue or problem in a city or a particular community: gun violence, rampant crime, gangs, public education, and the like. And the answer (or non-answer) is always the same: more laws, more police, more government, more regulations, etc. These questions and answers in my view continue to perpetuate these problems, not solve them, as we should have learned by now.

First, the proposed solutions of more laws, more police, and more academic studies of social problems, have proven to be ineffective for many years now. Secondly, politicians and the federal government have never been the solution in solving community problems. As Peter Drucker, the renowned businessman and "godfather of the nonprofit organization," said many years ago:

> Since WWII...the majority in all countries...believed that government should and could supply the community needs of an urban society through "social

programs". We now know that this was largely delusion. The social programs of the last fifty years have, by and large, not been successes. They certainly have not filled the vacuum created by the disappearance of the traditional community. The needs were certainly there. And so has been the money. But the results have been meager everywhere...The chaotic jungle into which every major city in the world has now degenerated needs, above all, new communities. And that, neither government, nor business can provide. It is the task of the non-government, non-business, non-profit organization. (18)

Thirdly, it is not the job of the President of the United States to provide solutions or be expected to fix the problems in local communities. That is not what we elect the President to do. Solving community problems is the job of the mayor, city council, county government, local police department, businesses, faith-based organizations, schools, and state government when necessary. In other words, local problems need to be solved by local community leaders, be they politicians, police, principals of schools, pastors, or volunteer parents.

The local citizens live there, work there, and care the most about what type of environment they and their families live in. They are in tune with and in touch with the heartbeat of the community. Given the opportunity and proper resources, local community leaders will resolve most community problems over time. To be sure, I'm not saying every single problem will always be completely solved. Solving community problems requires hard work, compassion, and leadership from dedicated individuals living in those neighborhoods.

I know of what I speak not only because I have done it myself, but also because after founding and being the Executive Director of a national nonprofit intermediary for twenty years, providing funding and capacity-building to local faith- and community-based nonprofits meeting the needs of individuals and families, (19) I understand the nuances and difficulty of dealing with communities and healing individuals and families. Thus, I am not speaking from theory or suggesting a "pie in the sky" solution. But what I am saying is that it is a mistaken notion that the federal government and/or President of the United States should be expected to solve local community problems, and we must stop giving our citizens that expectation of the President. It goes back to what President John F. Kennedy said in his 1961 presidential inaugural speech, *"Ask not what your country can do for you, ask what you can do for your country."*

All the above said, the most important element, force, and keys to building healthy and safe communities are parents. Parents are the most important people to help both solve and prevent community problems. Why? Because their role, their influence, plays a vital part for the future of the community. As I stated earlier, the neighbors in a neighborhood, the students in the schools, the entrepreneurs and employees of businesses, and citizens of the community come from the home. And therefore, who we send into the community every day is who we raise at home. The family is our best and first line of defense against negative influences. The home is the best place for prevention and intervention governance, keeping communities healthy, happy, and safe.

Finally, I believe every era has those extraordinary men and woman who will rise to the challenges of their time. It is my contention that the extraordinary men and woman of our time who must rise up to take on the complex challenges of this time, more than any other single entity, institution, or community program, are parents. That's why I call them, *Parents on a Mission!*

Prevention from choosing a negative lifestyle is not a matter of keeping our children from ever being touched by any or every negative experience available in today's American culture. No, our challenge is not one of isolation, but one of infiltration. Infiltrating the hearts and homes of the hopeless with parent heroes! As one minister put it, *"What counts in life is not being a hero to a guy two thousand miles away, but being a hero to a kid who is nine years old and two bedrooms away."*

I leave you with this one story I always share at the end of POM classes and training that exemplifies the core principle of what Parents on a Mission is all about. It beautifully sums it all up.

A Father, a Son, and an Answer

Passing through the Atlanta airport one morning, I caught one of those trains that take travelers from the main terminal to their boarding gates. Free, sterile, and impersonal, the trains run back and forth all day long. Not many people consider them fun, but on this Saturday, I heard laughter.

At the front of the first car—looking out the window at the track that lay ahead—were a man and his son. We had just stopped to let off passengers, and the doors were closed again. "Here we go! Hold on to me tight!" the father said. The boy, about five years old, made sounds of sheer delight.

I know we are supposed to avoid making racial distinctions these days, so I hope no one will mind if I mention that most people on the train were white, dressed for business trips or vacations—and that the father and son were black, dressed in clothes that were just about as inexpensive as you can buy.

"Look out there!" the father said to his son. "See that pilot? I bet he's walking to his plane." The son craned his neck to look. As I got off, I remembered something I'd wanted to buy in the terminal. I was early for my flight, so I decided to go back. I did—and just as I was about to re-board the train for my gate, I saw that the man and his son had returned too. I realized then that they hadn't been heading for a flight but had just been riding the shuttle. "You want to go home now?" the father asked. "I want to ride some more!" "More?" the father said, mock-exasperated but clearly pleased. "You're not tired? "This is fun!" his son said. "All right," the father replied, and when the door opened, we all got on.

There are parents who can afford to send their children to Europe or Disneyland, and the children turn out rotten. There are parents who live in million-dollar houses and give their children cars and swimming pools, yet something goes wrong. Rich or poor, black, or white, so much goes wrong so often. "Where are all these people going, Daddy?" the son asked. "All over the world," came the reply. The other people in the airport were leaving for distant destinations or arriving at the ends of their journeys. The father and son, though, were just riding this shuttle together, making it exciting, sharing each other's company.

So many troubles in this country—crime, the murderous soullessness that seems to be taking over the lives of many young people, the lowering of educational standards, the increase in vile obscenities in public, the disappearance of simple civility. *So many questions about what to do.* [Emphasis mine] Here was a father who cared about spending the day with his son and who had come up with this plan on a Saturday morning. The answer is so simple: parents who care enough to spend time, and to pay attention and to try their best. It doesn't cost a cent, yet it is the most valuable thing in the world.

The train picked up speed, and the father pointed something out, and the boy laughed again, and the answer is so simple. (20)

End Notes

Introduction

1. America's Children: Key National Indicators for Wellbeing, 2019 https://www.childstats.gov/pdf/ac2019/ac_19.pdf
2. Changing Course: Keeping Kids Out of Gangs https://www.ncjrs.gov/pdffiles1/nij/244146.pdf
3. In November of 1990 I was hired as the At-Risk Counselor at Santa Barbara Junior High School. In 1992 I transferred to the Santa Barbara High School so I could maintain my case load with the same students after they graduated from SBJH.
4. Miller, Alice. The Untouched Key, Tracing Childhood Trauma in Creativity and Destructiveness. Anchor Books, Doubleday, New York 1988.
5. In 2012, I implemented my POM training program in the Kern County Lerdo jail facility in Bakersfield, CA and later in 2015 throughout most of the prisons

in the Colorado Department of Corrections. To this day POM is used in these institutions, as well as the Pennsylvania Department of Corrections, and other correctional and institutional opportunities are on the horizon as of 2024.

Chapter 1 Parental Personal Growth

1. Friedman, Edwin H., et al. A Failure of Nerve: Leadership in the Age of the Quick Fix, Church Publishing, 2017. p. 249.
2. The POM mentor training is a three-day training I provide for community leaders that teach the POM curriculum in their respective communities. For more information: www.parentsonamission.org
3. Covey, Stephen R. Spiritual Roots of Human Relationships, Deseret Book Company, 1970. pg. 14.
4. Gibson, Lindsay C. Adult Children of Emotionally Immature Parents: How to Heal from Distant, Rejecting, or Self-Involved Parents, New Harbinger Publications. 2015, 1.
5. Gibson, Lindsay C. Adult Children of Emotionally Immature Parents, 177–196.
6. Goleman, Daniel, Emotional Intelligence: Why It Can Matter More Than IQ, Bantam Books, 1995.
7. Bess, Michael, Our Grandchildren Redesigned: Life in the Bioengineered Society of the Near Future, Beacon Press, Boston, MAm 2015, 81.

8. Canfield, Jack, The Success Principles: How to Get From Where You Are to Where You Want to Be, HarperCollins, New York, NY, 2005, 229.

9. I don't remember when and where I either heard or read this quote.

10. Stonehill, Robert, N, Wise and Shine. Edition 1, 14, 15. Copyright @ 2019 Robert N. Stonehill. In an effort to keep things simple, doable, and avoid making parents feel overwhelmed with information and "more stuff to do," I do not get deep into the weeds about the human mind. The subject of the power of our mind, our thoughts, and "thinking about our thinking" has been studied and written about by many. You could go to the self-help section of any bookstore or on Amazon and find many more resources than I am giving you here and I highly recommend it for those wanting to learn more on this subject. Stonehill's book, Wise and Shine is but one example.

11. Zinsser, Nathaniel, The Confident Mind: A Battle-Tested Guide to Unshakeable Performance, Harper Collins, NY 2022, 166.

12. Frankl, Viktor, Man's Search For Meaning, Washington Square Press, Pocket Books, 1959, 1962, 1984, 86. In Part I of his book Dr. Frankl describes the horrors of daily life in the concentration camp but then asks this all-important question about human liberty in the face of extreme environmental factors.

13. Ramos, Richard, From the Margins to the Mainstream: Preparing Latino Youth for Leadership in The 21st Century, Xulon Press, 2014, 79–81. I discuss some of

the domestic violence incidents I suffered as a child in this section of the book, so I won't go into detail here. I also talk about how though my father had passed away when I was eighteen years old, I came to realize that he, a dead man, was controlling my life and it wasn't until I forgave my father that I was able to overcome being a victim of my past.

14. Mandela, Nelson, A Long Walk to Freedom, Back Bay Books, Oct. 2013.

15. When I was the at-risk counselor at Santa Barbara Junior High School (and later at SB High School) I learned from my students how many of them felt their parents were still angry with them weeks, months, and in some cases, years after they had done something wrong. Thinking they were not forgiven made them feel ashamed, rejected, and abandoned—not wanted at home. I saw how this was at the root of so many of their dysfunctional relationships with their parents and a big reason why I started Parents on a Mission.

Chapter 2 Authoritative Parenting

1. Gibson, Adult Children of Emotionally Immature Parents, 2015.

2. "Millions of parents became rightly concerned that replacing reading, math, and science with, as one example, role-playing exercises on gender stereotypes might have a profound effect on the quality of their child's education. Some parents who spoke

up were shouted down, silenced, and even arrested for demanding answers about what schools were teaching. The National School Boards Association compared parents to terrorists....Books with highly sexualized and pornographic material were found in school libraries. Two California teachers allegedly tried to brainwash a student into changing genders behind her mother's back. A Tennessee school board told parents not to eavesdrop on virtual classes." https://www.texaspolicy.com/parents-have-every-right-to-know-what-their-kids-are-being-taught.

3. Neufeld and Maté, Hold on to Your Kids: Why Parents Need to Matter More Than Peers, Ballantine Books. 2014, p. 76.

4. This example took place many years ago with three of my now adult children.

Chapter 3 The Home Field Advantage

1. Haven, Kendall, F. Story Proof: The Science Behind the Startling Power of Story, Libraries Unlimited, 2007, 24.
2. Shreeve, J. "Corina's Brain" All She Is...Is Here." National Geographic, March 2005.
3. Miller, Alice, The Drama of the Gifted Child, Basic Books, 1997, 28–29.
4. www.First5California.com/parents
5. Miller, Drama of The Gifted Child, pp. 28
6. Friedman, Edwin, H. A Failure of Nerve, 182–3.

7. Ibid. p. 75.
8. Siefert, Katherine. How Children Become Violent: Keeping Your Kids Out of Gangs, Terrorist Organizations, and Cults, Acanthus Publishing, 2006, XVI, XVII.

Chapter 4 The Proper Use of Discipline

1. Neufeld, Maté, Hold On to Your Kids, 294–5.
2. Ibid., 199.
3. Schumacher, Kurz, The 8% Solution: Preventing Serious, Repeat Juvenile Crime, Sage Publications, 2000.
4. I say "as far as I know" because I have never seen or heard from others who teach this aspect of discipline. If there are others teaching these principles, I'd be happy to be proven wrong.
5. https://en.wikipedia.org/wiki/Susanna_Wesley.
6. Those of you younger parents probably don't know of Ann Landers. She was a newspaper columnist who gave practical advice to people who would write to her back in "the day" as us baby boomers say. This is a quote out of a book. However, it's a page I copied, and I no longer have the book to reference it here.
7. Cialdini, Robert, Influence: The Psychology of Persuasion, Harper Collins, 2007.
8. Amen, G. Daniel M.D., Magnificent Mind at Any Age: Natural Ways to Unleash Your Brain's Maximum Potential, Harmony Books, 2008.
9. https://www.care.com/c/france-has-officially-made-spanking-illegal/

10. https://www.ncbi.nlm.nih.gov/pmc/articles/ PMC3900086/ This is only one example of many demonstrating that much published research is biased.
11. https://www.wklaw.com/are-you-violating-california-law-if-you-spank-your-child/ This reference addresses California law. Laws on spanking probably differ from state to state.

Chapter 5 Building Safe Communities

1. This story was shared with me by a friend. I looked but could not find a reference for its original source.
2. Sinek, Simon, Start with Why: How Great Leaders Inspire Everyone to Take Action, The Penguin Group, 2009.
3. Jane Waldfogel, What Children Need, Harvard University Press, 2006.
4. Putnam, Robert D, Our Kids: The American Dream in Crisis, Simon and Schuster, 2006.

Chapter 6 Reconciliation

1. The Prodigal Son is a Biblical story found in the 15th chapter of the Gospel of Luke.
2. Barclay, William, The Daily Study Bible, 204–205.

Chapter 7 How to Win Loyalty

1. https://freebeacon.com/latest-news/school-district-bans-parents-from-board-meeting-on-policy-restricting-parental-rights/
2. https://nypost.com/2023/08/18/nj-school-districts-suffer-legal-setback-in-fight-for-parental-rights-against-state/
3. https://thepostmillennial.com/teacher-vows-to-keep-secrets-about-kids-mental-health-from-parents
4. Christopher F. Rufo, America's Cultural Revolution: How the Radical Left Conquered Everything, Broadside Books, 2023, 2.
5. Ibid. p.163.
6. Ibid, p. 166.
7. Jillian Peterson and James Densley, The Violence Project: How to Stop a Mass Shooting Epidemic, Abrams Press, 2021, 115.
8. Neufeld, Maté. Hold Onto Your Kids, 102–103.
9. https://www.discovery.org/education/2022/06/29/schools-are-stealing-parental-rights-causing-irreversible-harm-to-children/
10. Neufeld, Maté, 254.
11. Fischer, P., Sauer, A., Vogrincic, C., Weisweiler, S. (2010). "The Ancestor Effect: Thinking About Our Genetic Origin Enhances Intellectual Performance," European Journal of Social Psychology DOI: 10.1002./ejsp.778
12. I say age of ten and older, but this is only a guideline. Parents can decide at what age they want to include their children in this type of discussion.

13. I never personally met Mr. Covey but, as with so many of those I consider my "book-mentors," I diligently studied all his books and cassette tape series (I know… remember what those were?) and adopted many of his life principles he taught and wrote about, including The Seven Habits of Highly Effective People, probably his most well-known book.
14. Family Mission Statement exercise adapted from Stephen R. Covey, The Seven Habits of Highly Effective Families.
15. If your kids are at the pre-teen or teenage years it's best to discuss the day, time, place, and purpose for the family meeting with them to ensure their buy-in.
16. I developed this mission statement with my children when they were all relatively young, but I would say it still speaks to what we have tried and continue to try and live although they are now all adults on their own and some with their own children.
17. I want to say, "will always choose," but there are exceptions for both good parents and neglectful parents. Sometimes children of parents who do a good job still choose a negative lifestyle, and sometimes children of parents that were neglectful or abusive can turn out great.
18. Drucker, Peter F, The Community of the Future, The Drucker Foundation, Jossey-Bass Publishers. 1998, 1.
19. In July of 2003 I founded the Latino Coalition for Community Leadership, a national intermediary non-profit with the purpose of addressing the inequality of funding Latino-led nonprofits. Over the course of my

tenure (which ended in July 2023) we granted over $105 million dollars to more than 220 nonprofits in numerous cities in several different states. For more information: www.latinocoalition.org

20. Greene, Bob, A Father, a Son, and an Answer, Condensed from Chicago Tribune, Readers Digest.

About The Author

Overcoming the obstacles of barrio youth gangs, drugs and violence, Richard R. Ramos has devoted his career to serving high-risk youth and families.

To that end, in July 2003 Ramos founded the Latino Coalition for Community Leadership (LCCL), a national nonprofit whose purpose is to find, fund, form, and feature nonprofits in marginalized communities meeting the needs of individuals and families. Over his twenty-year tenure (July 2003 – July 2023) the LCCL granted over $105 million dollars in grants to over 220 grassroots nonprofits in numerous cities in several different states.

Ramos has previously authored three books: *Got Gangs? (2006)*, *Gang Prevention and Schools* (2008), and *From the Margins to the Mainstream: Preparing Latino Youth for Leadership in the 21st Century"* (2013).

In addition, he is the author and founder of "Parents on a Mission" (POM), a parent leadership program developing parent mentors who teach parents how to build healthy relationships with their children. POM has been adopted by school districts, nonprofits, the Colorado Department of Corrections, the Kern County (California) Sheriff's Office, and most recently the United States Agency for International Development (USAID) as part of their strategy for violence prevention in Guatemala.

Ramos has served as a correctional officer in California state and federal prisons, Juvenile Hall instructor, at-risk high school counselor, co-founding director of a gang intervention/prevention community coalition, director of a Latino youth and family teen center, and a founding executive director of the Interfaith Initiative of Santa Barbara County.

For his decades of community service and his work in the field of human rights, he has received numerous accolades and awards including recognition by the White House Administration, the United States Congress, the California State Assembly, and the Santa Barbara Hispanic Chamber of Commerce. He has been inducted into Morehouse College's Martin Luther King, Jr. International Chapels board.

Richard is father and stepfather to eight children, eleven grandchildren, and one great-grandchild. He lives in Santa Barbara, CA with his wife, Christina.

For more information about Parents on a Mission:
richard@parentsonamission.org
www.parentsonamission.org

Printed in the USA
CPSIA information can be obtained
at www.ICGtesting.com
JSHW021709240324
59781JS00001B/47

9 781977 268839